Johnny Cash

HOUSE OF CASH

THE LEGACIES OF MY FATHER, JOHNNY CASH

JOHN CARTER CASH

INSIGHT 👁 EDITIONS

San Rafael, California

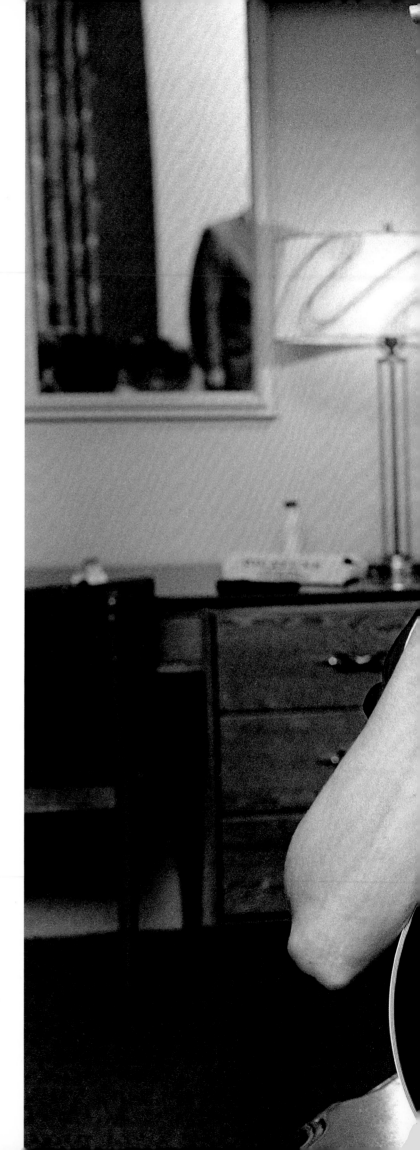

PAGE 1 | *The first page of one of my father's many notebooks. Dad was always writing and always protective of his ideas.*

PAGES 2–3 | *Beneath the tough exterior that Dad would project, he was a kind, gentle man.*

PAGE 4 | *My mother always said Dad wore black because it helped hide the stains.*

RIGHT | *My father, shortly after he signed with Columbia Records in 1958.*

FOLLOWING PAGE | *Dad and dear friend and fellow fisherman Johnny Horton, not long before Horton's accidental death in 1960.*

Pages 106, 131, 141 © Martyn Atkins; pages 128 (middle and bottom), 136, 159 (bottom) © Laura Cash; pages 25, 119, 130, 139 © Daniel Coston; page 124 © Annie Leibovitz/ Contact Press Images; pages 11, 121, 133 © Jim Marshall Photography LLC; pages 19, 127, 142, 146 (top left), 156 (bottom right) © Alan Messer Studio; pages 85, 147 © Lauren Moore; page 27 courtesy Sid O'Berry; page 128 (top) © Tony Overman; pages 59, 79, 82 (bottom), 86–7 © Regan Pictures, Inc.; pages 6–7, 8, 42–3 © Sony Music Archives. Photo Credit: John Hamilton; pages 101, 109, 110 © Sony Music Archives. Photo Credit: Don Hunstein; page 159 (top) © Marty Stuart

INSIGHT ⬬ EDITIONS

PO Box 3088
San Rafael, CA 94912
www.insighteditions.com

Library of Congress Cataloging-in-Publication Data available.

 REPLANTED PAPER

Insight Editions, in association with Roots of Peace, will plant two trees for each tree used in the manufacturing of this book. Roots of Peace ROOTS of PEACE is an internationally renowned humanitarian organization dedicated to eradicating land mines worldwide and converting war-torn lands into productive farms and wildlife habitats. Together, we will plant two million fruit and nut trees in Afghanistan and provide farmers there with the skills and support necessary for sustainable land use.

Manufactured in China by Insight Editions

10 9 8 7 6 5 4 3 2 1

CONTENTS

CHAPTER ONE

FRUITS OF THE SPIRIT

MY FATHER WAS A COMPLICATED MAN. THERE IS NO DENYING THAT. HE WAS A MAN OF STEADFAST FAITH AND AN OPEN BOOK IN SO MANY WAYS. BUT HE WAS ALSO A VERY DEEP AND EVEN MYSTERIOUS MAN, INTRIGUING AND UNPREDICTABLE. SOME MAY HAVE ARGUED THAT

he was defined by his failures, struggles, addictions, and pains. Kris Kristofferson called Dad "a walking contradiction, partly truth and partly fiction." He could not have been more aptly described. But the things that made him great were not these contradictions.

I feel it is important to share facets of my father's nature that are unknown to many of his fans. He was in many ways a simple man, giving and loving. He was brought up by a devout but nonjudgmental Christian family, the very salt of the American earth. He was creative throughout his life and not only with music. He was a poet, painter, photographer, humorist, cook, and fisherman—to list only a few of his talents.

I see my father through the world's eyes quite often, and to me there is much missing in the common perception of the man. To some he is the ultimate image of cool. His tough, haggard image is alluring and intriguing, and punks

and rockers around the world appreciate him as much as country music fans. However, beneath the surface there is much more. This book offers a deeper understanding of who Johnny Cash really was, beyond the illusion.

At the same time, there is really no way I could completely explain my father. I do not comprehend him fully myself and don't believe anyone alive does. Within these pages may be found a better understanding, but not a definitive solution to the mystery of exactly who he was. While so much is easily understood, the deeper one looks into Dad's life, the more perplexed one may become. With his songs he mesmerizes us, and with his dark and seemingly magical eyes he confuses us. But I feel this happens only when we lose sight of the simple defining characteristics that made up the man.

ABOVE | *My father was a gentle man—in every walk of life.*
OPPOSITE | *Dad literally carried me around the world with him through the early years of my life.*

DON'T MAKE A MOVIE ABOUT ME
Christmas 1982   J.R. Cash

If anybody made a movie out of my life
I wouldn't like it, but I'd watch it twice
If they halfway tried to do it right
There'd be forty screen writers workin day & nite
They'd need a research team from uncle Sam
And go from David Allen Coe to Billy Graham
It would run ten days in the final cut
And that would mean leaving out the gossip smut
And I do request for my childrens sake
Dont ever let 'em do a new re-make
The thing I'm sayin' is, dont you see,
Dont make a movie 'bout me
            Even for T.V.
Dont make a movie 'bout me

Dont let 'em drag old Hickory Lake
For my telephones and bottles and roller skates
Down forty feet in the cumberland mud
There's a rusty old gun that once shed blood
Out a hundred yards from my lakeside house
Weighted down with a rock is a skirt
                                    a blouse
A dozen pair of boots that made a dozen corns
Trombones, trumpets, harmonicas and horns
And the tapes that I threw from the lakeside door
Silverstein, and Kristofferson from years before
Everything has a story that should be let be
So dont make a movie 'bout me

Neither of my parents ever threw anything away. They gave things away all the time, amazing gifts on occasion, often on a whim to a loved one—beautiful guitars, suits of clothes, automobiles, all sorts of things. But throw anything away? Never. They had a storage vault in their office that they continually added to through the years, until it was full to capacity by the ends of their lives. After my parents passed, it became our job to go through these items and catalog them. I must give thanks to my wife, Laura, for her dedication to this daunting task, and to all who helped along the way.

There were master tapes dating from the mid-1950s through the early 2000s; there were also guns, clothes, railroad spikes, film reels, saddles (both for horse and camel),

THE ARTIFACTS OFFERED A CLEARER VIEW OF **WHO MY FATHER REALLY WAS.**

sketches, paintings, dried flowers, folders of song lyrics, bags filled with cassette tapes, stack after stack of quarter-inch audio tape mixes, strange hats, guitar cases (both empty and containing guitars), harmonicas, various piles of blank stationery, microphones, press promotion photos, phonograph records and players, and innumerable family, personal, stage, and random photographs. This list could go on and on.

Among the items we combed through were some treasures of great personal value. The songs, poetry, and other writings; the images; and the artifacts offered a clearer view of who my father really was. It became my mission to share what I felt he would have liked people to know about him. That is the essence of this book.

OPPOSITE | *My father was a modest man and at one point didn't much like the idea of a movie being made about him. Later on, Dad and Mom actually began the production of* Walk the Line *themselves, though they both passed away before its release in 2005.* ABOVE | *In the photo to the left my father is twelve years old. The other two are from one of my grandmother Carrie Cash's photo albums: The top photo is of Dad with his sister Louise, the one on the right is my father with his brother Roy (center) and uncle Horace Rivers (left).*

I have never forgotten one night late in the fall of 1974, in Davenport, Iowa. I was four years old. Dad stood beside me onstage, holding my hand and larger than life. My hair was red, unlike his, although my eyes were the same deep brown. I wanted to have black hair back then, wanted to be like him in every way. I could smell the alligator leather boots he wore. They were almost as tall as me, laced up to the knee and glowing with the sheen of many fevered rubbings. Dad loved his black shoe polish. He'd developed the habit of polishing his own boots during his time in the air force and continued it his whole life. He kept shoe polish in almost every drawer in his closet, in the cabinet beside his bed, and in his toiletries bag.

Onstage I could almost see my reflection in those boots. I was wearing my stage overalls, hand-embroidered with rainbows and a farm scene by my mother. She was onstage also, and we were singing "Can the Circle Be Unbroken." It was a song from her family—the Carter Family—and we sang it on every show. I bellowed loudly into my microphone. My pitch was bad back then. I could hear the melody, but without formal training, staying in tune was something else. Still, I sang with every bit of energy I had.

From the moment I could walk, my parents brought me onstage. They stood me in between them, gave me the mic, and told me to sing along. That night when the song ended, Dad turned to me.

"Thanks to John Carter for helping us with that one!"

The crowd roared. I felt the familiar bloom of joy inside. I loved the applause. It was addictive.

"Where are you going now, John Carter?" the man at my side asked, the entertainer, my father, and my idol.

"I'm going fishing," I answered.

OPPOSITE | *One of the things that made Dad so special as an entertainer is that he truly loved the music and the crowd.* TOP | *Here Dad is in a white shirt, which actually wasn't all that uncommon, despite his alias, "The Man in Black."* ABOVE | *When I was very young, Dad would bring me onstage for a bow each night at the end of "A Boy Named Sue."*

"You got worms?"

"Yep, but I'm going anyway."

The crowd burst into laughter. My one joke. It was always a hit.

Dad turned to the bandleader, Bob Wootton. "Bob, kick off 'Daddy Sang Bas—'"

"I've got a song I want to sing," I said loudly into the microphone. Bob looked at me questioningly. Dad turned to me, uncertainty in his eyes.

"Well, all right then," he said, after just the shortest of pauses. I chanced a glance at my mother; she was smiling, but had the same uncertain nervousness in her gaze.

I turned to the expectant crowd and sang, "I keep my pants up with a piece of twine, I keep my eyes wide open, I keep the ends out for the ties that bind, because you're mine." At that point I paused for effect, looking around. All eyes were on me. "I pull the twine!" I finished. The crowd did not disappoint me with their response.

Bob hit the first lick of "Daddy Sang Bass" on his guitar, but I called out loudly, "Wait! Wait! I've got another song!" My father turned to me with an unfamiliar stern gaze. I paid no heed. I glanced at my mother. She also eyed me incredulously. Bob stopped playing, looking to my father for direction.

The crowd had grown quiet. I had their attention.

"I'm being swallowed by a boa constrictor, a boa constrictor, a boa constrictor. I'm being swallowed by a boa constrictor, and I go down, down, down . . . Oh no." I looked at my father for support. He responded with a half smile. "There goes my toe. Oh, me—there goes my knee. Oh, fiddle," I wrapped my arms around my waist, tightening them, "It's up to my middle. Oh heck—it's up to my neck!" my hands around my neck. "Oh, dread—it's up to my . . ." at this I broke off into a garble of unintelligible sounds. The crowd once again laughed, but this time not with the same enthusiasm as before.

"That was wonderful, son," my mother said this time. "Now here we go! 'Daddy Sang Bass'!"

Bob again kicked off the song. "Wait! Wait!" I cried. "I've got another song!" My father looked at me sternly. It

DAD LET ANGER AND FRUSTRATION DRIFT AWAY FROM HIM WITH EFFORTLESS CALM.

was that same look I was unfamiliar with. His frown froze my words in my throat. My mother walked over to me and put her arm around me. My father, looming over me like a great oak tree, put his great hand on top of my little head, applying gentle but steady pressure. This time, Bob did not stop.

After the song, I headed to the dressing room with Mom. "Wait here for your father," she said. "I know he will want to talk to you. You were a bit out of hand onstage tonight, son."

"I was just wanting to sing a song, Momma."

"Well, there is a time for that, and you had your song. You were trying for too much. Now you just sit here and wait. Your dad will come see you after his encore."

So I sat and waited, anticipating what was to come. Waiting was the worst part of all. I listened first to the hypnotic drone of "I Walk the Line" and then the thunderous rumble of "Orange Blossom Special," Dad's harmonica wailing through it.

After the song ended, the applause died as the house lights came on. I heard the steady beat of those giant boots pounding down the hall, step by great step, toward the dressing room. I'd never feared my father, but I knew that I was in trouble then, and with each step, my heart beat harder until it was pounding in my ears in time with the thumping of those boots. The footfalls stopped outside the dressing room door.

Then the door handle turned, and slowly the door opened. There stood my father, looking huge. I cowered. He walked through the door and over to me. Then he kneeled on one knee, the sweat from the three-hour performance thick on his face and dampening his clothes. He moved close to me, his nose almost touching mine. We were eye to eye.

"Never. Never do that again," he said quietly and without anger. Then he smiled.

Dad let anger and frustration drift away from him with effortless calm. He never remained angry with me, never raised his voice to me except on rare occasions, and it was usually only to get my attention and keep me from hurting myself.

OPPOSITE | *My father always had a deep sense of peace and connection to God. His music and faith were especially important to him in his later years.*

When I was growing up, we spent a great deal of time in New York City. My parents had an apartment at 40 Central Park South, a penthouse overlooking the park. One day we were leaving the apartment, bound for Greenwich Village and Dad's favorite guitar shop. We climbed in our normal hire, a burgundy stretch limousine. As we weaved through traffic along the park toward Fifth Avenue, there came a sudden and unexpected crash. An entire window burst into a thousand pieces. Tiny shards of glass exploded everywhere, covering my mother and myself. Though we were all in shock, my mother sat still and did not scream.

"Is everyone alright?" called the driver from the front.

"I'm okay," answered my mother.

The car came to an immediate halt, and I saw my father reach and grab something from the floorboard—a sizable rock. He burst from the door and rushed to the sidewalk.

I moved toward the open door to follow, but my mother stopped me. "Stay still, son," she commanded as calmly as possible. The broken glass was all over her, though she did not seem to be hurt or bleeding at all.

A tall, shirtless young man was standing on the sidewalk, his eyes glazed over and his face blank. My father's face reddened with anger and he rushed up to him.

"Is this your rock?" he demanded.

The man began to jabber in a language I did not understand. There were a few English words mixed in, but not many.

I saw my father stand there, staring into the stranger's eyes. For a brief moment, I wondered if Dad was going to hit him, perhaps with the same rock the man had thrown through our window. But Dad only stood there, eye to eye

with the tall foreigner. Then Dad held out the rock again. "Take it," he said.

The man stopped talking and reached out his hand and took the rock.

"Go put this back where you found it, please," said my father, and then turned his back and walked to the car.

By this time, my mother and I had brushed off most of the glass. Except for a few tiny nicks, we were untouched.

"Good Lord, John. I am uncut. It is a miracle. What on earth was wrong with that young man?" My mother's grace was evident from her calm tone.

"I think he was on drugs, June," answered my dad. "I don't even think he knew where he was, much less that he threw a rock at somebody's big red limo."

I looked out the window and saw the man sitting on the curbside, staring down at the rock in his hand as if it had magically appeared there.

"Let's pray for him," said my father. "Stay in the car, son."

And so my mother and father got out of the car and walked over to the man. He looked up, not seeming to recognize my father as the same person who had just handed him the rock. I saw my father bend down on one knee, and then my mother with him. As they prayed, the man closed his eyes and began to cry.

Now when I think back and remember that day, I find a great lesson. My father showed that man immediate forgiveness and tenderness. There was never a moment's hesitation on Dad's part once he realized the man was confused and in pain. My mother was right beside him.

My father was a gentle man.

NYC APT 40 Cen Pk S.
Nov 17-18-19-20
1. Interviewed Ed M°Curdy
Songwriter. Secured new
songs from him and
signed him as House of
Cash writer.
2. Appeared at Madison
Sq. Garden.
3. Dental Appointment.
4. Bought Stage Clothes.
5. Made plans with
Marshall and Rick Humbard
Jr. to design and buy
new Sound System for
concert tours.
6. Phone Arrangements with
Jack Lauth on equip-
ment for Publishing Co.

OPPOSITE | *In the early 1980s, my parents had an apartment in New York City at 40 Central Park South. My father, mother, and I spent a fair amount of time in Manhattan.* ABOVE | *This is a short diary entry from the early 1980s, where Dad noted what he had been doing in New York over the past few days.*

while for window shopping and T.V. watching.

On Sunday morning we were still tired however from the previous tour. Not feeling like getting dressed for church we put on our blue jeans and walked down 5th Ave. We walked across the street to go around a large crowd about to go into a presbyterian church ~~Daddy look at that~~

We had been to the Calvary Baptist church once before, but today I didn't feel like public worship.

"Daddy, look at that church" said John Carter, pointing to St. Michaels Catholic Church. "Its so pretty," he said. "Whats it like inside?"

After a moments hesitation I said "Come on son, I'll show you."

We all found ourselves in the beautiful sanctuary, admiring the stained glass and feasting on the new found spirit of quiet reverence.

"Lets pray," said June. We knelt at a bench for silent prayer

Feb 14 '87

June,
Valentines is fine
But you being mine
is more fine.

Thine,

John

s
for
our l
saw it b

Valen
worked muc
late morning,
ing one of my mo
homemade biscuits.
milky-pink concoction
not seen Dad yet that morn

I was beginning to wonde
noon, when I heard his footsteps
stockinged feet gently padding along
long since he'd had surgery on his knee,
tiously. He walked into the kitchen, an item i
was a small package, wrapped in shiny red paper an
bright crimson ribbon. The other was a folded piece o
blue paper, my mother's favorite color.

Mom turned to him and smiled. "Happy Valentine's Day,"
he said, and handed her the card. She opened it and gazed
upon the inscription within. I leaned over between bites and
took a quick look. It was a simple design, just a statement of
his love for her, but her eyes lit up with a blaze.

"Oh, honey, I love you," she said, and he bent and
hugged her.

Then he handed her the package. She flipped open the top
of the box and inside found a ring with a shiny stone, deep red
and so bright it almost hurt my eyes.

"That's beautiful, John," she said, and slid the ring on her
finger. She put on her glasses and stared into its ruby depths.
Then she did the most curious thing: She took off the ring
and put it back in its box, sat it down beside her plate, and
picked up the card again. She opened it and once again read

OPPOSITE | *Dad never hesitated to take the time for prayer and to follow any direction he felt God was pulling him. Here, he tells how we wandered into St. Michael's in New York City one day when I was young.* ABOVE | *My parents in the late 1960s on a visit to the cotton fields near Dad's childhood home in Dyess, Arkansas.*

the words. I noticed the light in her eyes was much brighter when she looked at the card than when she focused on the ring.

The greater gift was the handmade card. And he gave her one every year. Even though the cards were often accompanied by a diamond necklace or some other piece of precious jewelry, it was the creative work that she was most touched by.

He never stopped writing to her, sending her love notes and letters. She cleared his spirit so many times of the dust and darkness, the anger and pain that often engulfed his life. He knew inside—though at times he obviously forgot—that she was more than he deserved, that she was his only by some grace God had provided him. And when he did forget, it was only temporary, and he would always remember again. And he would write to her.

Dad adored my mother. He cherished her as his greatest jewel, the way a shallower man would have cherished great riches. Dad would have cast all else aside at any time to keep my mother.

When my mother died on May 15, 2003, my father began to sell or give away all his possessions. Without her, nothing physical held any value to him anymore. His greatest treasure was gone.

My dad identified with the Old Testament character Job, who lost all. Dad was also familiar with suffering. He had chronic problems with his knee, beginning in the 1970s after he fell in an open boat well. He had three ribs broken once when a pet ostrich kicked him while attempting to disembowel him. After Dad broke his jaw in 1990, he had a bone graft, but the nerve did not heal right. It left him in chronic pain for the last thirteen years of his life. Like Job,

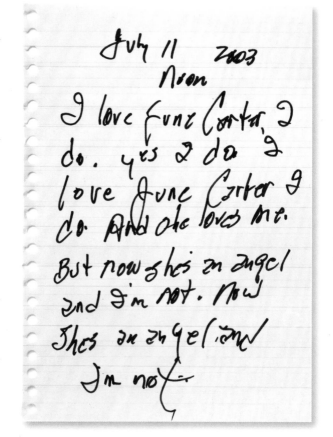

I believe Dad never cursed God, but rather came to accept his burden as best as a human could.

Dad "owned his pain," as he told me once. He was continuously hungry for spiritual wisdom, and the one subject on which he focused more than any other was the Bible. When his pains—both physical and psychological—bore down on him, he went deeper into his study of the scriptures. He was always looking for a better understanding of life and the troubles that came along with it. Whether they were struggles in his career or broken bones, Dad used these obstacles as stepping-stones to a greater spiritual understanding, a means of becoming closer to God. He once wrote, "The Master of Life's been good to me. He has given me strength to face past illnesses, and victory in the face of defeat. He has given me life and joy where others saw oblivion. He has given me a new purpose to live for, new services to render, and old wounds to heal."

When Dad suffered, he turned to music as well as to the Bible. Despite his setbacks, he never ceased working. In 1993 he began what I will argue was his most impressive and significant body of work, the records he made with producer Rick Rubin. Why his most significant work? Throughout his later years, his physical ailments were unending, but he never gave up. The pain was always there. His respiratory sicknesses came and went. He was in and out of the hospital all the time. He suffered from a neuropathic condition akin to Parkinson's disease, which the doctors initially diagnosed as a rare condition called Shy-Drager Syndrome. Later this diagnosis was discounted and it was determined he suffered from a condition known as autonomic neuropathy. Still, he never gave up. He continued making music and writing.

ABOVE | *Dad's love for my mom only grew stronger after she passed away.* RIGHT | *My father used to call my mother "June Love."*

Hey June,

That's really nice June. You've got a way with words and a way with me as well.

The fire and excitement may be gone now that we don't go out there and sing them anymore, but the ~~fra~~ ring of fire still burns around you and I, keeping our love hotter than a pepper sprout.

Love John

Dad retired from the road in 1997 because of this disease and intended to slow down. But he did not. It seemed that his restlessness only grew with his newfound idle time. He went back into the studio again and again. One week he would be in the hospital fighting another battle with pneumonia; two weeks later he would be finishing up what would become another Grammy-winning CD. From the time he retired until the last week of his life, he worked on his music. Without a doubt, his greatest suffering came after

THE MUSIC WAS HIS THERAPY, HIS SOLACE.

my mother died. But even then he did not stop, but instead redoubled his efforts.

I remember clearly, though through the haze of grief, the day of my mother's funeral. It was one of the longest days in my life, and most assuredly the longest in my father's. We left the grave site that day in a long stretch limo, my father and I along with my sisters. When we were barely out of the cemetery, Dad turned to me.

"I am ready to go in the studio, son," he said with haggard conviction. "I need to," he said.

OPPOSITE | *Dad never ceased to remind my mother of his love for her.* ABOVE | *This photograph was taken onstage at the Carter Fold in Hiltons, Virginia, in 2003. Dad seldom took to the stage after retiring in 1997. This was his next to last public performance.*

Mon

July 13 2015

Tremor: Tried to play
guitar. Maybe a little progress
I suppose that any activity
is a little progress

I cant draw pictures
Except for my standard
Micky Mouse.

Hello
I'm
Micky
Mouse

"Are you sure Dad?" I asked. My sisters heard him say this and looked on in surprise. "Are you sure you don't want to wait a week or so?"

"See if you can set up a session in three days," he said with tired determination.

And so in three days time we were in the studio. The music was his therapy, his solace. But it was so much more to him. In the music he found strength and purpose, and through the music he grieved more truly. Behind his final musical works was an almost preternatural persistence. His eyes were blind, his body was failing, but he pressed on.

It is one thing to make a great body of work while you're strong and in your prime. It is another to create such a body of work while battling suffering and sickness, continuing on through these storms with the determination of a captain at the helm of a great ship in a hurricane.

Dad's spirit did not give up. His body lost its ability to carry on, but if he had been able to, he would still be making music today. I have been asked if my father died of a broken heart. Certainly his heart was broken when he passed. But this did not kill him. His fortitude was inviolable, though his body would not last.

In sum, if I were asked to say exactly who my father was, I would answer that he was a gentle, loving, and persistent man. Oh, yes, there is so much more to who he was. Many knew him to challenge authority, and he was famous for his devil-may-care attitude. His compassion for the down-and-out marked his music, which has touched the lives of many people, without a doubt. All around the globe and in all walks of life, one can find his fans. An elderly farmer from Topeka, Kansas, is just as likely to have a comprehensive collection of Dad's music as a punk rock fan from Hamburg, Germany. His influence is far-reaching, to say the least. But Johnny Cash had the most profound hold on the hearts of those who were closest to him.

How can it be demonstrated that he was gentler than he was angry, more kind than forceful, more meek than boastful, and more loving than spiteful? How can I express the affection and support he gave to his loved ones, the faith he shared, and the spirit of giving he possessed?

How will Johnny Cash be remembered? As a face on a web page, an image across a screen and only the memory of his voice from a digital file or the rust of tape? As the resounding tones of a baritone voice or the defining sound of his boom-chicka-boom across the acoustic strings of his Martin D-28? Will he be remembered by a music video where he digs back through a painful past and reflects in pain the sufferings and hurts he lived and caused? Are all these true pictures of the man? Yes, in part. Most certainly.

But my father was so much more.

So let me share what memories and insight I have into who the man was beyond the song, and what the contours were of the spiritual and creative world in which he lived. As you turn these pages, I hope you will discover the man I knew—the father, friend, and man of God.

OPPOSITE | *Even during darker times, my father's humor and spiritual connection endured. He had drawn Mickey Mouse since he was a young boy.*
ABOVE | *My father was a contemplative man.*

CHAPTER TWO

BEGINNINGS & FOUNDATIONS

J OHN R. CASH WAS BORN FEBRUARY 26, 1932, INTO A FAMILY WHERE FAITH WAS OF PARA-
MOUNT IMPORTANCE. GOSPEL MUSIC FED HIS SPIRIT AND WAS ESSENTIAL TO THE FORMA-
TION OF MY FATHER'S CHRISTIAN FAITH. HIS HOME WAS FILLED WITH GOSPEL MUSIC.

Each night the whole family would gather around the radio to hear the songs of Jimmie Davis, Sister Rosetta Tharpe, the Carter Family, and later, Hank Snow. The family's love for gospel music touched Dad's heart deeply and stayed with him his whole life.

Carrie, Dad's mother, had an old guitar and played just a little—only a few chords, really. But Dad told me the first music he ever heard came from her lips. Although life was hard in Arkansas for the Cashes, there was always music.

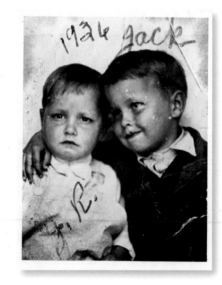

Dad wrote, "Babies get hungry if they aren't fed, and the babies of Ray and Carrie Cash were born into a world where times were mighty tough. But throughout the tough years of the Depression, up through the . . . thirties and forties, Ray Cash found honest work to feed his family."

In 1935 the Cashes moved from Kingsland, in southern Arkansas, to Dyess, in the northeast corner of the state. Their new town was a place of hope for farmers who had been granted land as part of Franklin Delano Roosevelt's New Deal. They all worked hard to make something of the dark earth, or gumbo, as it was called in that area.

I have often heard it said that my grandfather was a sharecropper, but that is not true. Under FDR's program, the farmers actually owned their land. In the spring the Cashes planted cotton seeds in the rich, black dirt. Come harvest, the entire family, young and old, picked the cotton all day, dawn to dusk, their fingers bleeding, their backs sore. "At times Carrie did this hard work while pregnant with another baby," my father wrote, "in order to help Ray Cash, who did every kind of labor known." And they sang through this labor, easing their souls. Most of the songs were from my grandmother's favorite southern gospel hymnal.

ABOVE | *My father's best friend as a boy was his brother Jack, two years his senior, who died at the age of fourteen.*
OPPOSITE | *My father's senior high school yearbook photograph.*

THE THINGS WERE
FRIGHTENED AT

WHEN I WAS JUST A LITTLE KID
AND PLAYED ALOT AT NIGHT
BACK IN OUR COUNTRY VILLAGE
WHERE WE DIDNT PAY FOR LIGHT
THEN I COULD SEE BEHIND EACH TREE,
AN INDIAN STANDING THERE
AND SAY, HOW I'D SHAKE AND HOLLER!
IT WOULD FAIRLY RAISE MY HAIR
AND WHEN I GREW TO BE A MAN
   I KNEW IT MORE AND MORE
THAT HALF THE FUN WAS KNOWING NOT
   WHAT I WAS RUNNING FOR
AND I USED TO GO TO TOWN
   EVERY NIGHT FOR PAW
I'D GO DOWN THE ROAD JUST, LICKEDY SPLIT!
   UNTIL MY FEET WERE RAW
I HAD A LITTLE COUSIN
   (HE WAS SCARY, TOO)
HE'S WORSE THAN I AM
   HE'S SCARED OF GHOSTS   ARE YOU
ONCE I HEARD MY COUSIN JUST OUTSIDE
   A YELLIN'
HE WOULDN'T TELL ME WHAT IT WAS
   I SAID THERE AINT NO TELLING

Very early on Dad showed great artistic potential, which can be clearly seen in his poetry and songs.

When my father was a boy, he and his brother Jack, who was two year older, were always together. Jack was Dad's best friend, and Dad looked up to him. Jack was strong and full of the love for God. He aspired at an early age to become a pastor and was on his way, studying the Bible daily.

"Jack never ceased praying," my father told me once. "His lips were continuously moving. I asked Jack what he was saying once, and he told me he was just talking to God."

In the summer of 1944, when my father was twelve years old, Jack suffered a tragic, fatal accident while working with a pendulum saw. When Jack died, my dad was visited by an angel.

I will never forget the way Dad disclosed this experience. We were traveling by bus across western Canada, en route from Banff to Vancouver. It was late summer, and the sky was almost clear. I saw wisps of clouds high above us and daydreamed about flying between them, looking for angels.

We were in Dad's private room on the bus, relaxing on the black leather couches as we barreled down the highway. "Dad, do you believe in angels?" I asked him.

"Oh, certainly, son," he replied. "I had a conversation with one once."

"Really, Daddy?" I asked. I was no more than ten.

Dad closed his eyes for a moment.

"Yes, son," he said, his eyes now focusing on mine. "After Jack's accident I couldn't sleep. So I would go out on the porch at night. When I sat down it was late afternoon, but I must have fallen asleep because all I remember was waking to the night. There was someone on the porch with me."

"Who was it, Daddy?"

"It was a man, son. Dressed in a gray suit," said Dad.

"Was it an angel, Daddy? Did he have wings?"

Dad smiled. "No, son. No wings. But I knew he was an angel." Dad picked up the Bible that always sat on the table in his private room and unconsciously leafed through the pages.

"I asked him," he said, "if he would take me instead of Jack. He said no, that it was not my time."

When I asked Dad if he had seen an angel since then, he said he didn't know for sure, but that he might have. And he continued to believe in them. I have been looking for them myself ever since that bus ride.

It took days for Jack to finally die as a result of complications from an infection. His death shattered my father, who

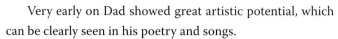
OPPOSITE | *Though Dad's life was full of hard work growing up in Dyess, Arkansas, he developed a wonderful sense of humor and made a habit of writing his thoughts down.* ABOVE LEFT | *Here Dad (bottom) has fun with friends A. J. Henson (middle) and J. E. Huff (top) during his early years in Dyess, Arkansas. The baby is Stanley Jones.* ABOVE RIGHT | *A sharply dressed young man (my dad's on the right) posing with a friend while on a trip to Memphis.*

But when I awoke the morrow morn
    I found this beggar gone.
And he left a piece of paper
    with these words so true and plain
"You have carried someone's burdens,
    you have not lived life in vain."
And if it was before me,
    I would do it o'er again
Just to help some weary pilgrim
And not live life in vain.

by

J R Cash
1948

was by Jack's side while he suffered. When Jack died, a part of my father almost certainly stopped growing in some way. Nevertheless, Dad matured a great deal through this experi-

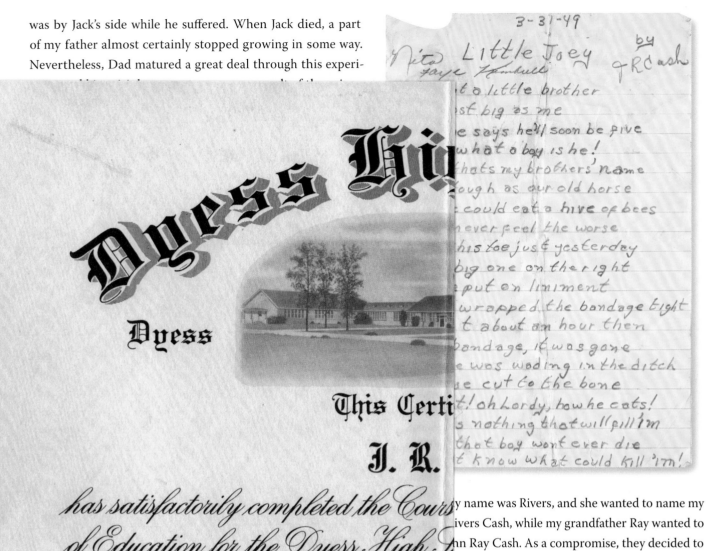

...y name was Rivers, and she wanted to name my ...ivers Cash, while my grandfather Ray wanted to ...nn Ray Cash. As a compromise, they decided to ...iddle initial instead of a middle name. This was ...n back then.

...ked the cotton fields all his years growing up; ...ard, like the rest of the family. His life consisted ...rk in the cotton fields in the afternoon, music ...ily radio in the evening, and the Saturday movie ...theater. The town of Dyess, albeit wonderful in ...held no future for my father.

...Dad had many great memories of his child-...me, it is evident that he could not wait to get out. ...id just that, joining the air force and taking an ...r to Germany. When he went to the recruiting ...oduced his birth certificate, the name on it was

The "R" did not stand for anything, and in discussing this with ... relatives, I discovered a mild controversy. My grandmother JR Cash.

Landsberger
December 10th

Dear Brother,

Since it came a blizzard, and I can't go out, I thought I might answer your letter that you wrote the other day, Nov 2nd.

And it did come a blizzard. I never saw anything like it in my life. I was on my way back from the PX this afternoon, minding my own business and this big black cloud came up, like it was gonna come one of them Arkansaw rains, but the sleet and snow hit all at once, and I almost lost my way before I got back. It's sure a cold, blue one, right off the north sea. Seventeen degrees is predicted for tonight, and colder tomorrow.

Right now, I'm on a three-day pass, but I think I'll wait till tomorrow to go anywhere, due to the weather. I'm going down to Garmisch in the Alps, and see if I can't break my neck on a pair of skis. Things are pretty cheap down there, so I hear, and plenty of free-hearted little people.

They changed my working schedule again today. From now on, I only work six hours a day, six days a week, with one three day pass per month. I'll be working from midnight to six in the morning, the biggest part of the time which is the best shift for my job. The

Only thing extra about this set-up is, I'll get two hours per day of Military training, and they do mean military training. I'm gonna get a little snow in my pants. I believe I'll like it though, might need it sometime.

Thursday, I went before the promotion board, and I think I'll know tomorrow whether I made it, or not. If I know the Air Force, I didn't, They like to see a man sweat, then give it to him the next month.

The black market has gone to the dogs over here. I can only get a little over double my money for cigarettes and coffee. When I first got here, I could get about 16 marks for cigs, and now they've gone down to about 13 or 14.

I guess you read about the big flood in Italy? A lot of the boys here want down there to help out, but I couldn't leave my job

Well, this is a good night for lots of things, and I don't have a choice, so I'm gonna hit the sack.

Tell the wife and kids I said "hello" and, Merry Christmas to all of you.

Love Brother
J.R.

THESE PAGES | *In this letter to his brother Roy, Dad shares his thoughts about daily life during his tour of duty with the air force in Germany. Dad was a high-speed Morse code interceptor who copied transmissions from Soviet Russia and all of the Eastern Bloc. At the time, his job was considered top secret.* LEFT | *Dad poses in his air force uniform.*

PNEUMONIA PARTY

DUE TO THE UNREST AMONG OPERATORS, IT HAS BEEN DEEMED NECESSARY TO TAKE MEASURES TO KEEP THE TROOPS HAPPY. SOME MEN WORK TOO HARD. ON SEVERAL OCCASIONS, MEN HAVE BEEN SEEN LEAVING THE OPERATIONS AREA WITH DITS AND DAHS HANGING OUT THEIR EARS, AND THEIR CLOTHES AND HAIR LITERALLY SATURATED WITH HAMMARLUND POWDER.

THE ONLY SOLUTION TO THIS IS TO LET THE MEN HAVE MORE TIME OFF. SINCE OUR SUPERVISORS THINK THIS IS IMPOSSIBLE, A PLAN HAS BEEN JERKED UP. THIS IS IT:

1. AT 0200 HOURS, NOVEMBER 18TH, ALL MEN, "TRICK A" WILL ASSEMBLE IN A SLOUCHY GROUP DIRECTLY ACROSS FROM THE SWIMMING POOL ON THE HIGH GROUND. (DONT COME IS YOU'RE DIT HAPPY)

2. DONT BOTHER TO WEAR CLOTHES. IF YOU'RE MODEST THEN WEAR A PAIR OF SHORTS, BUT YOU'LL NEVER CATCH PNEUMONIA THAT WAY.

3. THE TEMPERATURE SHOULD BE AROUND 20 DEGREES, BUT IF IT'S OUR MISFORTUNE FOR THE WEATHER TO BE WARM ARRANGEMENTS HAVE BEEN MADE WITH THE LANDSBERG ICE CO. FOR 1000 LBS. OF ICE WHICH WE WILL CHIP UP TO COVER OURSELVES WITH.

4. AFTER STANDING STILL FOR 30 MINUTES, WE WILL THEN POUR HOT WATER OVER OURSELVES AND SING "HEY GOOD LOOKIN" HANK WILLIAMS STYLE TO INSURE A SORE THROAT.

5. A MEETING WILL THEN BE HELD TO GRIPE. WE WILL ALL LIE ON OUR STOMACH IN THE SNOW (OR ICE) AND DISCUSS OUR SUPERVISORS, USING VILE AND PROFANE LANGUAGE, TELLING WHY WE DONT LIKE WHO.

6. S/SGT DRANE WILL BE REFERRED TO AS "DRAINO". ANYONE CALLING HIM S/SGT DRANE WILL BE GIVEN A COAT AND FORCED TO GO BACK IN WHERE IT'S WARM

7. AT THIS TIME WE WILL THEN RUN AROUND THE BASE AT TOP SPEED FOR 30 MINUTES. LATER WE WILL LIE IN THE SNOW (OR ICE) TO MAKE US COLD AGAIN.

8. WE WILL THEN CRAWL ON OUR STOMACH TO THE BILLETS, CLOSE ALL WINDOWS TURN UP THE RADIATOR, AND STAY SWELTERING HOT ALL NIGHT.

AFTER THIS A FEW OF US WILL PROBABLY CATCH PNEUMONIA. THOSE FAILING TO DO SO WILL HAVE TO FIND A MEANS OF THEIR OWN TO GET OUT OF WORK.

ANY MAN CATCHING DOUBLE PNEUMONIA WILL BE AWARDED (BY THE TROOPS) A ROYAL PURPLE SHAFT WITH TWO BARBED WIRE CLUSTERS.

WE HEREBY FREEZE OUR #*#£$ SEALS:

John Cash

CHAIRMAN OF THE JOINT CHIEFS OF COUGH.

Ted Freeman

SPONSOR OF PNEUMONIA PARTY

"You have to have a first name," the recruiter told Dad.

"John," my father answered, though few people had ever called him that. And so JR Cash became John R. Cash. He was a high-speed Morse code interceptor and was very good at what he did. Even later in life, he could still write and read Morse code, and proved it to me once by writing out the twenty-third Psalm in the staggered code of dots and dashes. I wish I had kept that piece of paper. I don't know what happened to it.

Dad was very creative during his time in Germany, and wrote an early version of what would become "Folsom Prison Blues" while he was there. He also bought his first guitar in Germany, near the base in Landsberg. Here is a comic piece that he wrote during that time:

THE FLIGHT BEFORE CHRISTMAS

'Twas the flight before Christmas, and all down below,
Not a thing was I seeing, not even the snow.
Visibility was zero, no stars were in sight.
It was promising to be a heck of a night.
The co-pilot was sleeping, but not in his bed
While visions of Broadway danced in his head.
The rest of the crew was just sitting around.
Thinking of life in the old home town.

And I, in my cockpit had set the controls
Hoping the fuel was going to hold.
When on engine "4" there arose such a clatter
I started checking the dials to see what's the matter.
And doing so, this instantly came to mind;
the R.P.M. was only half time!
With the old inter-com I yelled "Pilot to crew!
Number 4 is kapoot! You know what to do."
I opened the throttle on old number 4
But only three engines were making her roar.
So I set up the crate so she'd run on the three.
And told the Radio Operator to get on the key.
I knew that our field must be pretty near,
If it wasn't, then we'd never see the new year.
After minutes of sweating they finally came through
And said their visibility was zero, too!
So they picked us up with their radar eyes,
And started giving us intro to fly.
"Two degrees to the left, and keep on the line.
You don't see us, but you're coming in fine."
Drop her a little now, and drop her slow
There's just about 4 more minutes to go."
Altitude 300, you're coming in Roger!
The strip's just ahead, so buddy don't dodge her.
Visibility zero, I still couldn't see.
But thank God the G.C.A.* man saw me.
Then the final command "Gear down and roll!"
I rubbed mother earth, and we'd reached our goal.
When we came to a stop, and finally unpacked
I felt like Santa Claus opening his sack.
And when I crawled in my sack the end of the day,
I was thanking my God for G.C.A.
And I hear the boys say, when they turned off the light,
"Merry Christmas to all, and brother what a night!"

*GCA: GROUND CONTROLLED APPROACH

When my father completed his tour of duty in 1954, he did not return to Dyess. Instead, he settled in Memphis, Tennessee, and married Vivian Liberto. He loved Vivian dearly and had written her constantly while on his tour of duty. Dad tried a variety of jobs: He was a door-to-door salesman, and he worked with his brother Roy for a while in the auto industry. But his heart kept wanting more.

OPPOSITE | *Cold weather and hard work inspired Dad's "Pneumonia Party," in which he humorously makes the case that having pneumonia would be better than continuing his grueling work schedule in the air force.* OPPOSITE, BOTTOM LEFT | *While in Germany, Dad continued his writing (both poetry and songs), learned to play guitar, and played music with a variety of other musicians, on and off the air force base.* TOP | *He also took the opportunity to travel around Europe and visited Italy and France, among other countries.* FOLLOWING PAGES | *Eddie Hill, Dad, Porter Wagoner, and Hawkshaw Hawkins in Meridian, Mississippi, in 1957.*

Rosanne, Dad and Vivian's eldest child, was born in 1955. Three more girls, Kathy, Cindy, and Tara, followed Rose. Soon after Rosanne's birth, he began to work hard on his music. Dad was limited as a guitar player—and never believed otherwise. But there was something about his style that was special.

In 1954, Dad walked into Sun Records and right up to the producer, Sam Phillips. He introduced himself as John R. Cash and said he wanted to record gospel music. Dad sang a hit record for Sam by Governor Jimmie Davis, "I Was There When It Happened." Sam immediately saw the potential in my father, but he was not looking for a gospel singer. He told my dad to come back when he had some original material worked up. Dad did come back, with "Hey Porter" and "Cry, Cry, Cry." Sam signed him to Sun Records, where Carl Perkins and Elvis Presley, among others, were already on the roster.

In the 1960s Dad fell into an emotionally darker period. He struggled with a feeling of isolation, which was aggravated by the remoteness that comes with fame. Drug addiction also held a powerful control over his life. He spent countless hours in the desert alone. His home life with Vivian was in shambles and Rosanne, Kathy, Cindy, and Tara were suffering because of it.

Despite these personal difficulties, Dad forged ahead and broke new ground in music, his creative energy unabated. His concept albums *Ballads of the True West* and *Bitter Tears* were like nothing that had come before. It was after their release that the concept album took hold in popular music. Dad led the way, most certainly. Music was solace to him, just as it had been when he was a boy. He never lost his passion for it.

My father had first used drugs in the fifties, but it was in the mid-sixties that his addiction took a deeper and deeper hold on his life. I can remember when I was young, my father saw a photo of himself taken during 1966 and said simply, "That is a very sick man."

Dad hit a hard rock bottom sometime in the fall of 1967. The pills he was on stopped helping, and he nearly died. Those who loved him, including a strong and loving woman he had adored his whole life, offered great help. Finally, he managed to pull himself through and rededicate his life to Christ.

OPPOSITE TOP | *Dad tuning a twelve-string resonator guitar.* OPPOSITE BOTTOM | *Dad with Carl Perkins.* TOP LEFT | *My father onstage with the Tennessee Two (guitarist Luther Perkins and bassist Marshall Grant) in the mid-1950s.* ABOVE LEFT | *Dad with one of his longtime favorite performers, Ernest Tubb.* ABOVE RIGHT | *A great photograph from a late-1950s recording session.* FOLLOWING PAGES | *Candid photos taken at home with Vivian Liberto, my dad's wife at the time, in 1958 by Columbia Records photographer Don Hunstein, right after Dad signed with the label.*

To Mama & Pop,
All my Love,

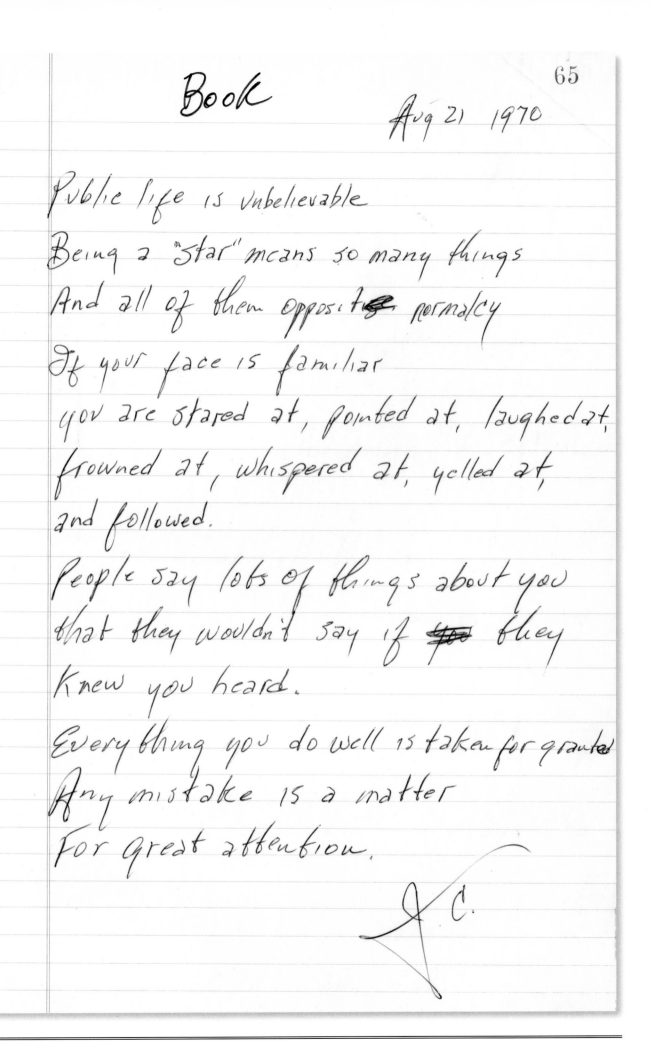

Book

Aug 21 1970

Public life is unbelievable

Being a "star" means so many things

And all of them opposite normalcy

If your face is familiar

you are stared at, pointed at, laughed at,

frowned at, whispered at, yelled at,

and followed.

People say lots of things about you

that they wouldn't say if ~~you~~ they

knew you heard.

Everything you do well is taken for granted

Any mistake is a matter

For great attention.

J. C.

OPPOSITE | *Because this photo is inscribed "To Mama and Pop," and is signed "John," it is most certainly a gift to my mother's parents, Maybelle and Ezra "Pop" Carter.* ABOVE | *My father was a regular, simple man in many ways. He never really struggled with fame, though at times it complicated his life.*

CHAPTER THREE

FAITH

& PHILOSOPHY

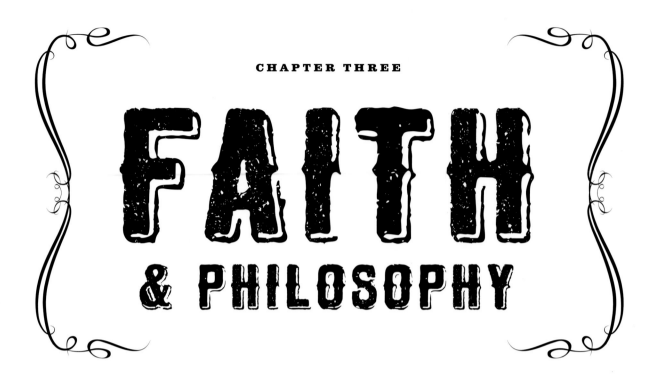

THE MAN I REMEMBER FROM MY EARLY CHILDHOOD WAS STRONG AND CERTAIN, CONSISTENT AND TRUSTWORTHY. HE WAS WIDELY FAMOUS BY THAT TIME, A HOUSEHOLD NAME, REALLY. HE AND MY MOM SPENT MUCH OF THEIR TIME TRAVELING THE WORLD,

and they took me with them. We traveled to Europe, Australia, Asia, and Africa. By the time I was nine, I had been to more than thirty countries, including the Holy Land and almost all fifty states, always by my parents' sides.

Dad had a great love for the Holy Land. I was but a baby on my first trip there, when he was making the film that he produced on the life of Christ, *Gospel Road*. Numerous trips to the Holy Land followed.

In 1977 Mom and Dad took a large group of people with them to Israel. They loved the people they employed, and they showed it by selling their Rolls Royce limousine and spending every penny from the sale on a two-week tour through the Holy Land for each and every employee, and most of the family— over thirty people. I will never forget that trip; we all grew closer together because of it. As for my parents, their relationship remained strong, their love true and clear.

My dad valued education—he was a lifelong student himself. So when I was six, he and my mom decided I should stay home so I could go to school during the fall and spring, when they toured. They employed Winifred and George Kelly to watch over me. These deeply spiritual people were kind and strong Seventh-day Adventists. They cared for me with deep devotion. For our family, home life was good and road life was an adventure. Dad was clear-eyed and spiritual, and it seemed as if his addiction was a thing of the past. This was the life I knew then.

The one thing that was constant in my father's life was his religious conviction. He remained a Christian man of faith, and from this he never strayed, eventually becoming an ordained minister. He was always willing to offer his testimony. Although the weight of stardom sometimes settled heavily on his shoulders, he would step up to the pulpit for this purpose any time. He

ABOVE | *My father introduced me to Billy Graham at a very early age. Billy was always gentle and caring.*
OPPOSITE | *Billy Graham and my father cherished their relationship and were as close as brothers.*

Hendersonville Tenn   May 26 1977

My son, John Carter attends
school regularly at ~~the~~ a Christian
school ~~he attends~~. It has been
a joy to see how well he has adjusted
to school, after traveling with June
and I for six years. He loves to
attend, gets along well with his
classmates, and for all practical
purposes, is just "one of the kids"
getting, nor requiring no special
attention because of his parents
"celebrity" status.

Recently though, he missed a
day of school due to a sore throat,
and on that particular day the girls
were pitted against the boys in
his class for a bible story memory
contest. The girls won.

But my head must have swollen
twice its size from pride when the
teacher told me, the next day that
one of the boys had remarked,
upon losing: "I'll tell you one
thing! I'll bet the girls wouldn't
have won if John Carter Cash
had been here!"

3 John 4. I have no greater joy
than to hear that my children
walk in truth.

believed it his duty as a Christian to share his salvation.

Dad was not a judgmental type of Christian. He was open to people from all religious denominations. My father focused on the Bible as the source of his own Christian faith and did not lean so much on the offerings of any denomination in particular.

Though Dad grew up Southern Baptist, he went to the churches of a variety of denominations through his life. In the 1960s Rev. Floyd Gressett of the Avenue Community Church in Ventura helped Dad find recovery and reaffirm his salvation. In the early 1970s my parents were members of Rev. Jimmie Snow's Evangel Temple in Madison. They would bring the whole family to worship there, including my sisters, whenever they were in from California. My mother's daughters, Rozanna and Carlene, came, too, as did good friends, such as Kris Kristofferson and Larry Gatlin. Jimmie's preaching was full of the spirit, and Dad and Mom were forever eager to sing

" I HAVE NO GREATER JOY THAN TO SEE MY CHILDREN WALK IN THE TRUTH. "

along to the music. But eventually, we left the Evangel Temple and became members at the Hendersonville Church of God, pastored by John Colbaugh.

Pastor Colbaugh was a dear friend to my dad, and it was at this church that I found my own salvation and was baptized at the age of nine. Dad was beside me that day and was thrilled. He often said, "I have no greater joy than to see my children walk in the truth." Another Christian brother and spiritual counselor was Rev. Jack Shaw, who traveled as part of our touring group in the middle to late 1990s through the last few years of the road show up until my father disbanded it in 1997. Jack was a gentle and wise man with a unique vision: to open a hospital in Nakuru, Kenya. Dad supported these endeavors, and the family still supports Jack's ministry today. Dad also gave his friend and advisor Nat Winston a lot of credit for his spiritual influence.

OPPOSITE | *After years of touring with my parents at a young age, I was enrolled in a Christian elementary school at the age of six. A spiritual foundation was of supreme importance in our household.* ABOVE | *This photo of Billy Graham and me was taken by my father from our boat. Billy and I are fishing from a friend's stilt house off the west coast of Florida. I was six years old.*

Dad had many who helped him along his spiritual path, true friends who did not want anything from him but to be his friend and support him when needed. These spiritual advisors were just a few of those who shaped his life. There were too many to mention them all, but undeniably one of my father's dearest brothers in faith was Dr. Billy Graham. Their friendship began in the 1960s, when Dr. Graham sent a message to my father. Billy later admitted that he reached out to Dad at first in order to impress his music-loving son Franklin!

"Johnny Cash called me on the phone," Billy told me. "I was amazed. He asked me if my wife and I would come spend the night with them. I said I'd be honored."

And so Billy and Ruth Graham flew to Nashville and spent a few days with my parents. They ate good food, laughed, and got acquainted. This trip began a friendship that would last a lifetime. Over the years, Billy and Ruth

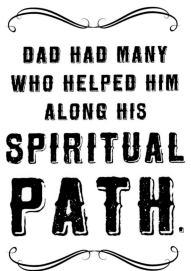

DAD HAD MANY WHO HELPED HIM ALONG HIS SPIRITUAL PATH.

and my parents spent a great deal of time fishing, swimming, relaxing—just being together. Dad and Billy studied the Bible together.

Dad was impressed by Billy's wisdom, but Billy was humble. As a boy I thought of him as a dear uncle. He was my fishing partner, too, and even helped me learn how to swim.

Dad took part in Billy's crusades year after year. He not only professed his faith with each appearance, but also spread his love for gospel music even more. He performed old standards along with songs of his own composition.

Dad stayed friends with Billy through the years. There wasn't an instance when Billy wasn't there to support him, especially through the bad times and even when he was in the throes of addiction. Just as Dad was nonjudgmental, so was Billy. They were a pair of great men, for sure. God had gifted both of them with talent and wisdom. But beneath all the

OPPOSITE AND ABOVE | *For years, my mother and father performed as a part of Billy Graham's crusades, spreading their testimony to millions of people around the world. As Billy was my father's dear friend, Ruth Graham (beside my mother in the photo opposite) meant the world to my mother.*

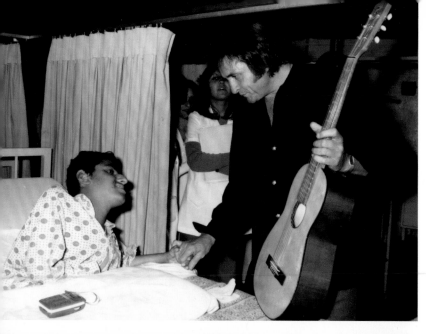

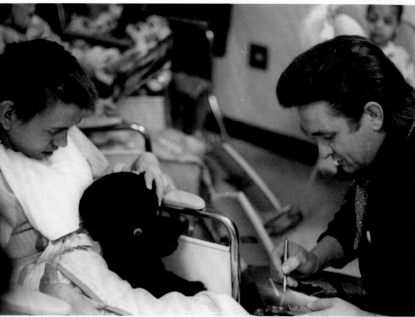

trappings of their fame were the simple hearts of good men. I had always been aware of this truth, but I sensed that perhaps there was something more, something I did not understand about the men and their friendship. A few years after my father died, I set out to understand this better.

On a cold January day in 2008, I visited Billy at his home in Montreat, North Carolina. We ate ribs and talked about his relationship with my father. I felt there must have been some great mystery to such a profound and influential friendship. Look at all the people they touched through the years. Billy performed the work of God, miraculous work, as far as I was concerned. And Dad had joined him in this endeavor.

"What was the nature of your deep connection with my father?" I asked him. "What made you connect?"

"We were Christian brothers," he responded simply.

"What did you first think of my dad when you met him?"

"My first initial impression of your father was surprise," he answered. "I did not expect him to be that ordinary. I loved your father. He was one of the few men who I have really loved."

And so we finished our dinner and talked about my father and my mother, about their time together. I began to understand that the secret to their great friendship was a resounding and simple truth: Both men were seeking to grow closer to God. They both had a great love for the Bible. There was no secret of a mysterious brotherhood, just faith.

When I drove home from Billy's that day, my belly was full, and my heart was overflowing with peace and understanding.

When it came to his faith, my dad used his celebrity as a platform to spread the word of Christ—and not just during Billy Graham's crusades. Dad never performed a show without singing gospel songs such as "Why Me Lord?" and "Peace in the Valley." Whether he was in the White House singing for a president or performing before hundreds of inmates at San Quentin, he never skipped the spiritual portion of the show. He got people's attention with songs like "Cocaine Blues" or "Folsom Prison Blues," his demeanor cool and dark. Then he professed his faith and sang of God and salvation. My father knew that along with all the great blessings he had been given came a great responsibility. So he used his fame to God's advantage by giving testimony.

ABOVE | *Dad never failed to take whatever time was needed to reach out to those in need, keeping his heart forever open to those who loved him. He truly cared about people. He never visited the sick or ailing for appearances, but because he felt that a great responsibility came along with fame and celebrity.*
OPPOSITE | *My father's inscription on the first interior page of one of our family Bibles.*

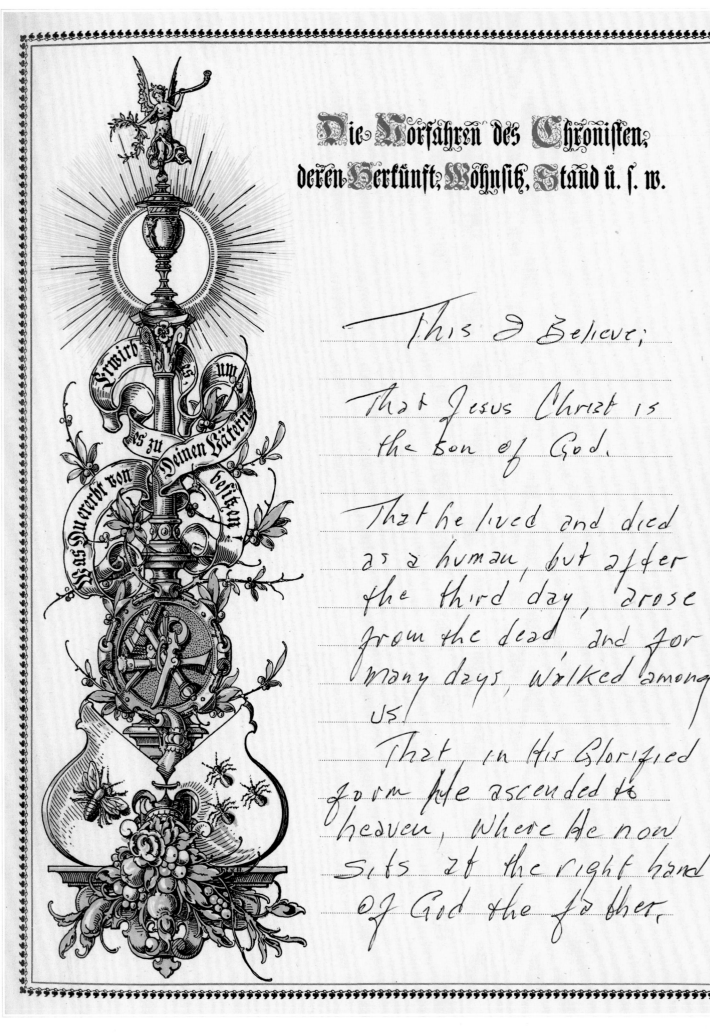

Die Vorfahren des Chronisten,
deren Herkunft, Wohnsitz, Stand u. s. w.

This I Believe:

That Jesus Christ is
the Son of God.

That he lived and died
as a human, but after
the third day, arose
from the dead, and for
many days, walked among
us.

That, in His Glorified
form He ascended to
heaven, where He now
sits at the right hand
of God the father.

L.I. New York   May 8 1977

For a long time I let my
status as a celebrity keep me from
a lot of public worship. Maybe I
used it as an excuse, (maybe I still
do at times) But one of my most
embarrassing moments was in a church
in a little town in Ohio.

I was on a tour of one niters
and found myself with a Sunday
off, enroute to Wheeling W.Va.
When I walked in the service all
but stopped. Heads turned and a
buzz went thru the congregation.

All I had wanted to do was
to quietly join a worship service,
sit in the back, unrecognized,
then just as quietly, leave when
it was over.

But the preacher recognized
me. Asked me to stand, I bowed,
got down. Then he asked me to sing.
I declined due to lack of acc-
ompaniment. Well, how about
sharing a testimony with us?"

Sometimes Dad's fame and lack of anonymity did get to him. He could not walk into a grocery store unnoticed. Once, while attending a public event in North Carolina, he tried a disguise of an orange wig and glasses. Everyone recognized him. He said later, "I didn't look like someone else. I looked like Johnny Cash in an orange wig and glasses."

I never saw my father be ungracious to his fans, despite the fact that he missed his privacy. People still come up to me and tell me of their interaction with my father and mother, how kind my parents were, and how they took the time to chat. Dad and Mom were always willing to hear fans' stories of their love for their music, no matter how trivial.

HE COULD NOT WALK INTO A GROCERY STORE UNNOTICED.

Dad had a great love for mankind in general. He not only felt this love but also showed it openly in numerous ways. When we were in New York City in 1980, the year I turned ten, I remember the cold wind blowing up and down Fifth Avenue. My mother was dressed in one of her knee-length mink coats with a matching hat. Dad was wearing a Western-style duster and no hat. We passed a man in scruffy clothes with a long, unkempt beard, who had passed out on the street. He smelled bad and I walked on past, but Dad stopped right beside the man. My mother, who was walking ahead with me, stopped also. Dad reached down and gave the man, who was regaining consciousness, a bill—a twenty.

OPPOSITE | *Dad never ceased to share his Christian testimony, although sometimes fame did complicate his search for silent prayer and deeper understanding.*
ABOVE | *I never saw my father decline a request for an autograph, even when his hands were full (with me, in this case).*

Omaha
TRAVELODGE
®

Tell Mama I'm proud of her,
and for her, that her album
is hung at the top of the
charts, but please give us
young punks a chance.
I'm kidding of course, but
Columbia says my new album
"Blood, Sweat & Tears" is already
their biggest seller. Your family
is mainly responsible for this
album and it's unusual sounds.
I'm always grateful.
Tell Mama much love
from me.
P.S.
John

I'm striving to remain properly adjusted

for June's back. I've taken her
to three different doctors,
and they all say she needs
to have traction on her leg.

I'm so proud for you, that
after all the wisdom you've
stored up, you going to tell
other people about it. It's
a wonderful vocation. I've
looked for the books for
you that you wanted, so
far I haven't found them
I'll come across some
thing that you'd want
sooner or later,

Hi Pop,

I certainly regretted that I couldn't come on to Nashville after June & were at Jackpot. But with the abscesses on my teeth, I would have been a burden on my friends, and have a bad recording session.

I'll be there in March no matter what. I can't do without that famous break- fast you cook much longer. We're all fine except

The man rolled over and a book fell from where it had been cradled against his chest as he slept. It was a Bible.

The man looked up at my father. "Thanks a lot," he said groggily. He looked at my father again with a start. "Man, you look just like Johnny Cash!"

"I get that all the time," said my father, smiling.

We walked away and I heard the man call back, "Thank you again, man!" I turned to look back and saw that there was another bill I had not noticed beneath the twenty. The face of Benjamin Franklin was evident on the crisp green note—a one hundred dollar bill.

Dad raised his hand in a casual salute.

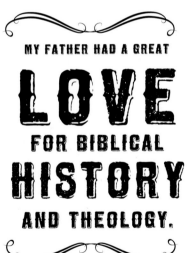

MY FATHER HAD A GREAT

LOVE

FOR BIBLICAL

HISTORY

AND THEOLOGY.

My father had a great love for biblical history and theology. In 1977 he studied with an organization called Christian International and obtained an associate's degree in biblical

studies. His notes were focused and thorough, and always annotated. Dad was dedicated to reading and studying, and throughout his life he read daily. His library was full of books, including one by Josephus, the ancient Jewish historian; *The History of the Decline and Fall of the Roman Empire*, by the English historian Edward Gibbon; and many others.

Dad's love of books was shared by my mother's father, Ezra. They developed a deep friendship in the 1960s, even before he fell in love with my mother. They corresponded regularly, keeping up with each other's studies and trading tidbits of knowledge. If my mother was my father's greatest love, his second was books.

When I look at my father's and grandfather's books now, I feel as if these bound volumes themselves hold power, and perhaps they do. With all the hours these two men spent toiling over them, making notes in the margins and wearing down

OPPOSITE | *This is a letter my dad wrote to my mother's father, Ezra "Pop" Carter, congratulating him when he became a minister in 1963, the same year that saw the release of his* Blood, Sweat and Tears *album and my grandmother Maybelle's* Mother Maybelle and Her Autoharp. ABOVE | *On visits to Cinnamon Hill, Jamaica, my father and mother would make time to care for orphans at the S.O.S. Children's Village in Barrett Town. My sisters Rosie (left) and Rosanne (middle) sit behind my dad in this photo.*

At Home   May 13th 1977

Christian International Univ
Conferred upon my self today an
Associates degree in Theology.

This "sheepskin" represents
my 60 completed Semester hours
over the past two and a half
years.

In my acceptance remarks
I said "lets dont make too
big of a deal out of this thing.
A christian has an obligation
and a privelege to study his
bible!

"I would liken this associates
degree to someon having just
finished the ~~~~ 9th grade
in school. I have just taken
one more step toward trying
to learn my bible. When I
graduate from high school, thares
Still ~~~~, college to go.

But it gets better all the
time. Digging into the Word

the bindings, perhaps some of their spirits dwell within the pages, comfortably resting on the shelves of my library. Perhaps they sleep here in wait of the Second Coming these two men so firmly believed in.

Dad had an insatiable hunger for new knowledge, continuously delving deeper into his studies. Through all stages of his life, even throughout his addiction, he kept reading and searching. In the 1980s, after a bout with pain-pill addiction, he decided to take on the daunting task of writing a novel about the conversion of the Apostle Paul. This book, *Man in White*, which was published in 1986, is a testament to my father's love of the Scriptures. He felt a kinship with the Apostle Paul, having been blind and misled for so long and eventually finding salvation. Although Dad's career was arguably at a low point during the mid-1980s, his drug addiction prompted him to search more persistently for his salvation.

OPPOSITE | *It is a little known fact that my father was an ordained minister and presided over a number of weddings, including my sister Kathy's.* ABOVE | *Dad and Mom often had friends over for what he called "guitar pulls." The guitar was passed around and everyone played his or her newest compositions. The conversation often took an introspective turn.*

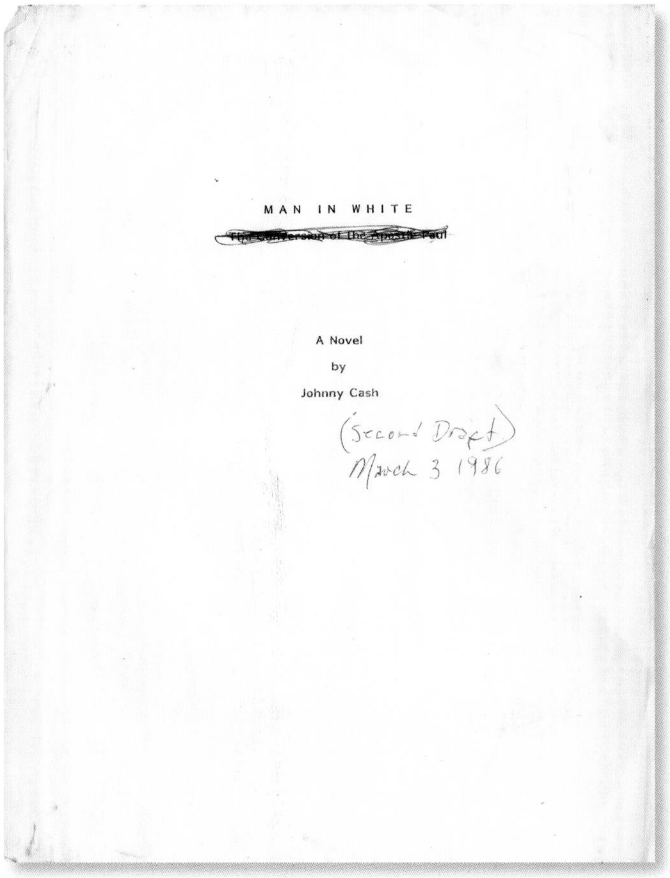

Page 1 (title page):

MAN IN WHITE
~~The Conversion of the Apostle Paul~~

A Novel
by
Johnny Cash

(Second Draft)
March 3 1986

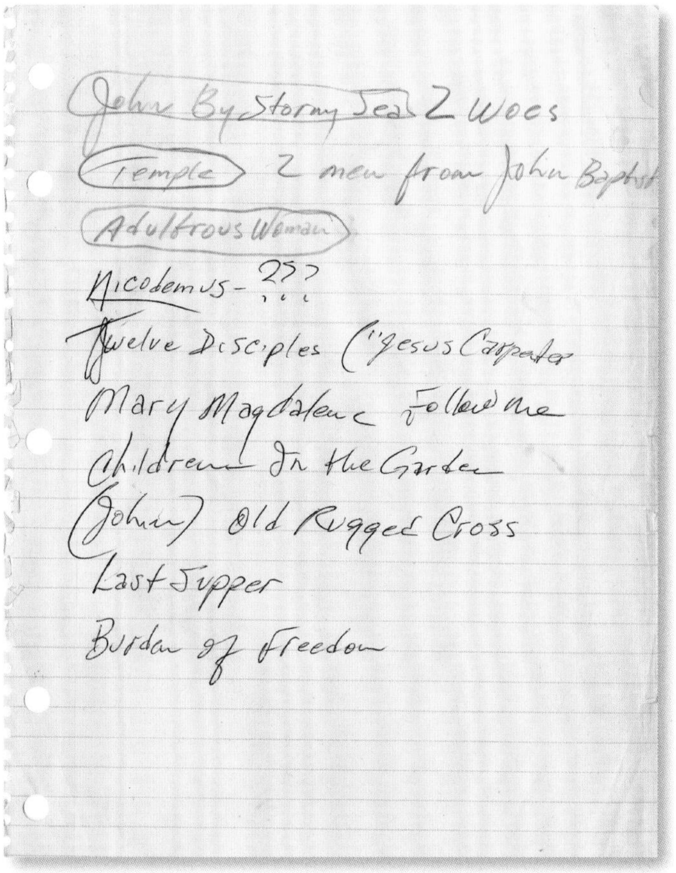

Page 2 (notes):

~~John By Stormy Sea~~ 2 Woes

(Temple) 2 men from John Baptist

(Adultrous Woman)

Nicodemus - ???

Twelve Disciples ("Jesus Carpater

Mary Magdalene Follow me

Children In the Garden

(John) Old Rugged Cross

Last Supper

Burden of Freedom

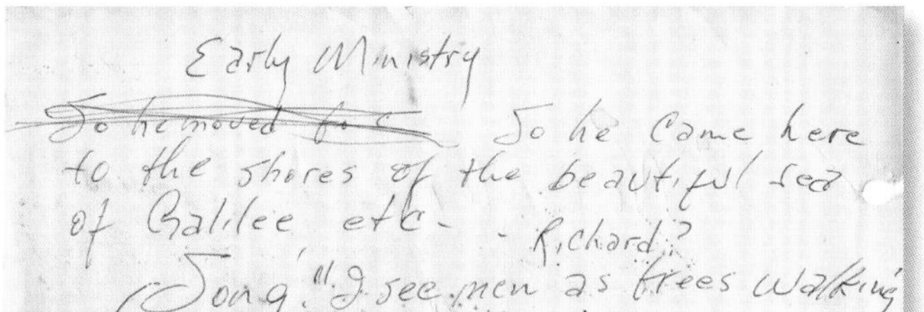

Page 3 (Early Ministry):

Early Ministry

~~So he moved to~~ So he came here
to the shores of the beautiful sea
of Galilee etc. - Richard?

Song "I see men as trees walking"
or
Song "2nd verse "Praise the Lord"

And he spoke to them in Parables
(Lessons on living in down to earth
Language (Lessons in justice mercy
compassion charity Love)
Good Shepard here...??? Brotherhood

Walk on Water here?
Parable of Sower?
" "
— The Greatest Commandments

↓ here

Then Cana Miracle

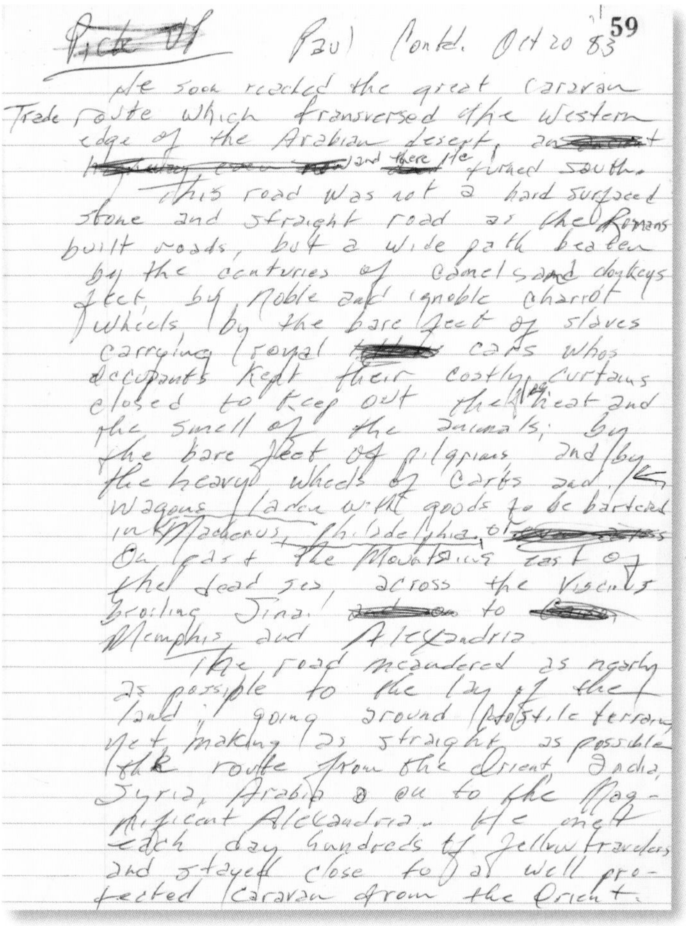

Page 4 (Paul, cont'd):

~~Pick up~~ Paul (contd. Oct 20 '83   59

He soon reached the great caravan
Trade route which transversed the western
edge of the Arabian desert, ~~an~~
~~the way can~~ ~~and there he~~ turned south.
This road was not a hard surface
stone and straight road as the Romans
built roads, but a wide path beaten
by the centuries of camels and donkeys
feet, by noble and ignoble charriot
wheels, by the bare feet of slaves
carrying royal ~~   ~~ cars whose
occupants kept their costly curtains
closed to keep out the heat and
the smell of the animals, by
the bare feet of pilgrims and by
the heavy wheels of carts and
wagons laden with goods to be bartered
in Madeurus, Philadelphia, ol ~~   ~~
On past the mountains east of
the dead sea, across the Negev's
broiling Sinai ~~   ~~ to
Memphis and Alexandria.
The road meandered as nearly
as possible to the lay of the
land, going around hostile terrain
yet making as straight as possible
the route from the Orient, India,
Syria, Arabia & on to the Mag-
nificent Alexandria. He met
each day hundreds of fellow travelers
and stayed close to a well pro-
tected caravan from the Orient

THESE PAGES | *Above are draft pages from Dad's novel,* Man in White, *in which he tells the story of the Apostle Paul's conversion to Christianity. Dad was a lifetime student of Paul, and he considered* Man in White *one of his most important accomplishments. While writing* Man in White, *Dad would carry the manuscript around with him in a pair of saddlebags (left).*

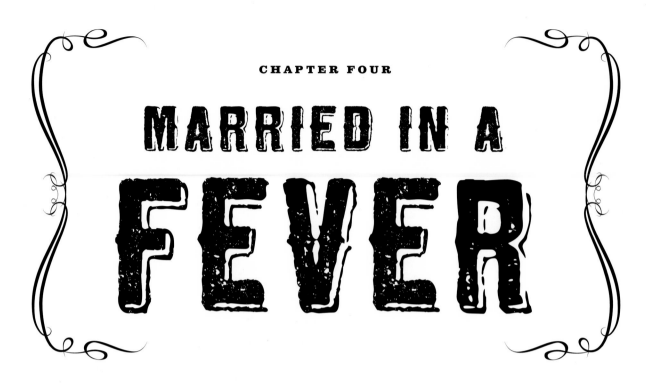

CHAPTER FOUR

MARRIED IN A
FEVER

F YOU WERE IN THE COUNTRY ON A WINDLESS NIGHT AND STOOD BY A BARBWIRE FENCE, YOU COULD HEAR THE RADIO," SAID MY FATHER. **"THAT WAS HOW STRONG THE SIGNAL WAS FROM THE TEXAS BORDER STATIONS."**

In the late 1930s and early '40s, a doctor named Brinkley set up an unbelievably powerful radio station, 500,000 watts, just over the border in Mexico. This was a massive signal, even by current standards, and was way over the allowed legal limit in the United States. It was from this "stage" that the world first heard the original Carter Family: A. P.; his wife Sara; his sister-in-law, Maybelle; and many more from the next generation, including Maybelle's daughters, Helen, Anita, and the energetic, rambunctious June. Literally, the entire United States heard these broadcasts. It was said that *The Carter Family Hour* was easily heard on radios as close as Memphis and as far away as Chicago and Los Angeles. It was on this radio show that a young JR Cash first heard June Carter sing and tell a few jokes.

After the first night he heard her on the radio, Dad told me, "I laughed

at her all the following day long. I was enthralled with her from the moment I first heard her speak."

Dad told me something else that I never forgot: "You know how when you hear someone's voice on the radio, you get a visual idea of what they look like? And when you see the person, they never look like you pictured them? Well, it wasn't that way with your mom, son." Dad smiled. "I had never seen a picture of June when I heard her on the radio, but when I did see a picture not long after, she looked exactly like I had pictured her, just exactly."

And so JR Cash sat and listened to June and her famous family on the radio, sang her songs along with her, and dreamed.

According to legend, when my father first met June backstage at the Grand Ole Opry in 1956 he

ABOVE | *As a child, my father listened to the Carter Family on the radio. Among the second generation of this illustrious musical family were my mother, June (middle), and her sisters Anita (left) and Helen (right).* OPPOSITE | *The day my father first met my mother backstage at the Grand Ole Opry, he told her he would someday marry her. At the time, he surely meant this as a joke, but he must have intuited that they were meant to be together.*

had been assertive and self-assured. "Hello, I'm Johnny Cash," he had said. "I'm gonna marry you someday."

Supposedly, my mother replied sarcastically, "I can't wait." She had just divorced Carl Smith, but my father was most certainly still happily married. Their brief encounter did begin a friendship, though.

My mother had one daughter, Carlene, with Smith. The year after their divorce, she married Rip Nix. They had a daughter, Rozanna, or Rosie as we called her. My mother and Rip became separated not long after their marriage, but they did not legally divorce until 1965.

In 1962 my father asked the lady who was one day to be my mother if she would go on the road with him and open the show with her music and comedy routine. Before there were any real sparks of love, there were definitely sparks onstage. When they performed together, Mom and Dad were magical. In 1964 they

BEFORE THERE WERE ANY REAL SPARKS OF LOVE, THERE WERE DEFINITELY SPARKS ON STAGE.

recorded their first duet, "It Ain't Me, Babe," a song by my father's favorite poet, Bob Dylan.

Dad was ceaselessly searching, forever yearning for something that he felt was missing. He was assuredly in love with my mother quite a bit earlier than he was willing to admit. They were both searching, really, and Dad saw the light of home and hope in my mother.

Their relationship, onstage and off, never ceased to be a roller-coaster ride. By the mid- to late 1960s, Dad's drug addiction was in full force. His drug of choice at the time was speed (amphetamines), though he took barbiturates, too. His isolation was a huge part of his sickness back then. He would disappear, sometimes for weeks, taking his RV into the desert to try and "find himself," as he liked to put it.

OPPOSITE | *Mom in full form as a character she created, Aunt Polly Carter.* TOP LEFT | *Mother Maybelle with the Carter Sisters.* TOP RIGHT | *Maybelle and the Carter Sisters with my father in the late 1960s.* ABOVE RIGHT | *Dad escorts Mother Maybelle and Sara Carter of the Original Carter Family into the Carter Family Fold in Hiltons, Virginia in 1975.*

July '55
Marietta.
Ark.

My mother and Marshall Grant, Dad's longtime bass player and road manager, struggled intensely with my father at the time, as did many others. Sometimes he was hard to deal with and unpredictable. Dad and his band were all very crazy on the road. They tore out walls in hotel rooms to make connecting rooms, shot out neon signs with their pistols, and more than once released hundreds of baby chickens into a fancy hotel lobby before fleeing. They really wrote the book on the rock-star life. But neither the drummer, W. S. "Fluke" Holland, nor Marshall ever drank or did drugs. As for the wise and quiet guitarist, Luther Perkins, he was often the brunt of jokes and mostly kept to himself.

My mother supported my father and was a great friend. Dad likewise appreciated her and her whole family. He brought her sisters Anita and Helen on the road with his show, and not long after, the legendary Mother Maybelle Carter joined them. Maybelle had never stopped playing music after the disbanding of the original Carter Family. She had continued to work with her daughters, playing at the Grand Ole Opry for years and spreading her family's music throughout the world. Now, on the road with Johnny Cash, the Carter

legacy only grew stronger. And in this great country music family, my father saw his future, his home.

I believe Dad carried a great deal of pain inside—pain and feelings of guilt about his rebellious lifestyle. And I think that was largely why his addiction held such a strong grip on the man. But along with the pain and guilt, there was faith. And in time, that faith would prove to be the strongest force.

TOP | *Here my dad is with the Tennessee Two, guitarist Luther Perkins (left) and bassist Marshall Grant (right). This is not long after he began to follow his dream of becoming a performing musician.* ABOVE | *Dad with Maybelle (front left), the Carter Sisters, and band members outside the walls of Folsom Prison in January of 1968. He holds my mother's hand, not two months from their wedding date.* OPPOSITE | *For much of his life, Dad had a great flame of dissatisfaction burning inside, although he was never far from friends and family, to whom he returned and who embraced him.*

Poem Written on Drugs
California desert 1965

Under a Manzanita tree
Sits a pencil, a piece of paper
And me.

John Cash

California Poems 1966

Theres trouble on the mountain
And the valley's full of smoke
There's crying on the Mountain
And again the same heart broke
The lights are on past midnite
The curtains closed all day
Theres trouble on the Mountain
The valley people say'

John Cash

But before there was any redemption and change for my father, he always had to reach a hard rock bottom, and sometimes that bottom was unbelievably low. As Dad described it to me later, he would hit bedrock and keep on digging. It was during the year 1967 that he was lower than he had ever been before, and he most desperately needed my mother. He had left Vivian by then, and he was touring with my mother. But she refused to become involved with him romantically because he was so drugged and crazy.

My father set off to visit some land he had purchased in southeast Tennessee near Chattanooga, a place called Nickajack Cave. He stumbled into the cave, stoned out of his mind, not really sure what he was doing, but clearly suicidal. Inside the cave over the next few hours he sobered up, and when he did, his suicidal notions abated with the high.

"I was scared out of my mind when I straightened up, son," he told me. "When I walked in that cave, only my guitar in my hand—not even a flashlight—I didn't know if I wanted to live or die. Then suddenly I was sober and knew for sure that I wanted to live. I wandered around for a long time in that cave, thought I was lost for good, that I would die there. And so I prayed. I begged God to let me find my way out. I promised Him I would change. It was not long after that I saw the light of the moon through the darkness."

When he came out of the cave, he still struggled with the drugs. But his love for my mother was unwavering. When he begged for her love in return, she gave him an ultimatum: "Either you straighten up, or I will leave the show and there will be no chance for anything between you and me." And so my father did that. He straightened up. Their love became strong, but I feel it never would have lasted if they had not experienced hardship and pain. For them complacency was as dangerous to their relationship as infidelity would have been. It was the uncertainty and excitement of it all that kept them interested.

And so my father, not long sober, asked my mother to marry him live while onstage in London, Ontario, the night of February 22, 1968. With the whole audience watching, he implored her to be his wife. And after some unstaged consideration, my mother finally said yes. I am eternally grateful that she did.

And so it was that two years after their marriage, almost to the day, I was born. At the time my father had a hit television show on ABC, and they brought me onstage in front of

the world. It was into this life I was born, the limelight and excitement of superstardom, and it was in this world that I searched, grew, and struggled beside them.

My father was a solid rock when I was a little boy. He had given up drugs and it seemed the darkness was all in the past. I remember seeing him onstage in Washington, D.C., in 1976, reciting his famous poem "Ragged Old Flag." Back then to me, my father may as well have been the president himself—strong and true and larger than life. But at the same time, Dad was a gentle and loving man, my best friend. He taught me not only about life on the road but also about the woods and nature. From my dad I learned how to hunt squirrels and fish at an early age. My father was not into competitive sports in the least, only outdoor activities. And beyond all that, he taught me about people, showing me that folks are mainly good, and that most can be trusted.

OPPOSITE | *The greatest love of my father's life was undeniably my mother, June Carter. When they married on March 1, 1968, Dad wiped the slate clean and started anew. Certainly this was one of the most important years in his life for many reasons.* ABOVE | *My parents' love for each other was indisputable and came through in their many performances together.*

Book 63

The Baby   *Sept 16 1970*

You can tell by the hair on my baby's head
That his mother is a thorobred

Cause he favors his mother more than he does
You can tell that she has a pedigree

You can tell from my little chip o' the block
That his mother must surely be royal stock

But the thing that thrills me thru & thru
Is, he favors his daddy a little bit too

Dad stayed close to Rosanne, Kathy, Cindy, and Tara, and they visited often, although all four of the girls grew up living with their mother in California. My mother's daughters, Carlene and Rosie, were both living in our home in Tennessee when I was born, however Carlene married Joe Simpkins in 1971, and Rosie married Scott Lawhead in 1974. So by the time I was four years old, I was living for the most part as an only child. My father loved all his children equally; there was no doubt about it. But his marriage to my mother and my birth brought him peace. It seemed he had found his place and for the time being stopped searching.

Dad treasured his time at home with his family. While we were apart during my parents' long tours, he would write me letters regularly. I recall waiting for my parents to return home on the scheduled arrival day from a long tour, waiting and waiting. When the door finally opened and I heard the fall of his footsteps, I would run to meet him. Dad's eyes were full of light and joy, always gentle.

Dad and Mom were late one winter night, traveling home by bus from Wisconsin. I am not sure what year it was, but I was young, maybe six or seven. A great storm had settled in, and the snow was blowing hard—three inches on the ground in Nashville, which for our southern town is a great deal. The locals were unaccustomed to this type of weather. I waited eagerly with Winifred Kelly, whom I called K, for their arrival. As the night wore on I grew more and more worried, but also increasingly sleepy.

TOP | *A poem about a six-and-a-half-month-old, me.* ABOVE | *I was born on March 3, 1970, two years after my parents' marriage.*

Finally, K put me to sleep in my bed, long past my bed-time. In the middle of the night I woke up, walked out of my bedroom and up to my parent's bedroom. It was still empty. Why weren't they home by now? I was afraid they had been in an accident. I looked outside and saw that it was still snowing. I sat down beside the front door and leaned my head up against the wall. Before long I drifted off to sleep.

When I awoke, I was back in my bed. I ran upstairs and found my parents asleep. I went to the kitchen where I smelled bacon cooking, and K at the stove. I saw two other people there I did not know.

It turns out the tour bus had gotten stuck at an exit ramp somewhere in Kentucky, its tires lodged in the deep, slushy snow. A couple driving a jeep had stopped to help them. When they realized it was my parents in the bus, they of course were surprised.

"We are trying to get back to see our son," Dad said.

"Well, we can take you," the man responded.

"That's a long drive," Dad said. "If you take us home, you will have to spend the night and eat breakfast with us."

And so it wasn't long until my parents came down to the kitchen, and we all ate breakfast. I remember those people were sweet and not pushy at all, or in the least bit starstruck. When we finished breakfast, they went on their way.

Dad and Mom were good-hearted, unassuming people. They had welcoming natures and offered their home in gratitude to these ordinary, helpful people.

Around 1979 something began to change, and though I did not understand it then, I do now. My father had begun to use drugs again and was struggling. The fights began, and I was usually right in the middle, literally and figuratively. The father that I had known as a boy began to dissolve into another man, who I did not know at all. Though the real John R. Cash, my dad, did come around quite often, "CASH," as my dad called him, also reared his ugly head with frequency. My mother's and father's love for one another altered and faded during these trying times, though it never disappeared.

One day during a particularly tough fight, I decided to shift the focus to me, as I did often. I ran outside while they were screaming at each other and called out, "I will never come back!"

I ran up a hill near our house on Caudill Drive in Hendersonville, Tennessee, and hid behind a bush. Within minutes my mother came up the hill.

ABOVE | *I never knew Tara (far left), Cindy (left), Kathy (right), and Rosanne (far right), my father's daughters from his marriage to Vivian Liberto, as half sisters, but only as whole ones. This feeling came from my parents, who wanted me to see no separation between us. Likewise, I have always felt the same way about my mother's daughters, Rosie Nix Adams and Carlene Carter.*

JOHNNY CASH

Rancho Mirag
B.F.C.   Co.
Dec. 21 198_

Hi Son;

I have achieved another step.
I am out of the Eisenhower Hosp
and into the Betty Ford Center.

I'm very happy here. They ar
keeping me busy with all the daily
and evening activities.

I want to a lecture this mor-
ing. It was on meditation. I
think I'm learning how to meditate

Definition; Meditate: "The listen,
half of prayer."
Isnt that neat?
Have a nice holiday son. I
love and miss you and mama.

Dad.

"Son," she said, "we are sorry you are having to hear this." She put her arm around me and I cried and cried. I walked back down to the house with her, where my father sat waiting. They did not fight any more that day.

Though the fights got worse before things got better, and though my mother almost left my father during that period, their love simply would not die. My father's addiction had a strong hold on him, and some days he was simply not there—I mean both emotionally and mentally. I remember worrying that they would get a divorce, a horrible fear to me, second only to their dying. Like most children, I thought of my parents and myself as a unit, a being in itself. I saw that unit crumbling, and I was terrified, fearing my father might die. And it was this ongoing dance of fear that made it so hard. One day they were together and I saw hope for our family, but soon they were fighting horribly. The cadence of their marriage was not consistent in any way throughout my early teenage years.

The bottom came in 1983, when my father went to a hospital for a surgery to remove a cyst from within his sternum that was threatening to block his esophagus. When he came around from that surgery, after almost dying, the family gathered around him and begged him to get treatment. He did so. He wrote me the letter shown on the facing page from the Betty Ford Center in Rancho Mirage, California.

Later in my life I also suffered from addiction. Many had assumed that after being so close to the darkness of my father's addiction, I would not fall prey to this sickness myself. Addiction holds no regard for the past, as we do. It was much greater than I was and took hold of my life completely, as it did my father's. Dad was one person when under the influence of drugs and another when he was not.

I believe most assuredly that Dad was a good man, a strong man, and a man of faith. But he was full of contradictions. Many times in his life, the dark side overshadowed his true nature. He would have been the first to say it was his selfish nature, the sinner inside, that was in a seemingly eternal battle for control. And though his faith was strong throughout his whole life, his darkness was forever his unwelcome companion, pulling him back into the same addictions and struggles.

So what pulled him through? Was it my mother's love for him, gentle and steadfast? Was it the fact that he had hit a hard bottom where his only chance of survival was to rise up? Was it his enduring faith in God? His desire to return to the fold and be that family man again? My belief is that it was all of these things.

It was the people in Dad's life, there to support him, who mattered. There were too many to do them justice here. There was never a time that Billy Graham wasn't there for Dad, always nonjudgmental, always caring. Larry Gatlin, Kris and Lisa Kristofferson, Waylon Jennings, Jessi Colter and Dad's sister Reba Hancock were also there for him, and, of course, my mother.

When Dad returned from the Betty Ford Center, he had a new lease on life, a new direction. Like the Apostle Paul, the scales were pulled from his eyes.

So much has been written about his sickness and addiction. But they did not make the man. Each and every time it seems diffused, the light within my father would come back,

OPPOSITE | *Though Dad struggled with addiction much of his life, he always picked up and regained his center. When I received this letter in December of 1983, I was overwhelmed with joy, even though it meant I wouldn't spend that particular Christmas with my father.* ABOVE | *My parents certainly had their struggles through the years, but their love remained strong. They always found their way back to each other. Their life was not necessarily "happily ever after," but rather "happy after all."*

and that is how I remember him best. Yes, the light shined through and triumphed in the end. And that light was brightest when it was enhanced by my mother's. She was strong and at the same time just as gentle as the breeze from across the mountains where she was raised.

My father adored my mother, always did. He was a hardheaded old-fashioned man, for sure. And there were times when he could be hard on my mother, though never physically abusive—never to her, and never to me or any of the family. I remember many times when I was young my mother would roll her eyes at me and say, "Your dad is a BEAR today!" But she had a way of softening his toughness, reducing his stress, and making life easier on him. In the process, she made life easier on all of us.

That gentle love Dad had for Mom was evident in the many letters he wrote to her through the years. And not only letters. Dad would give personalized gifts to her, perhaps a photo album with handwritten captions and anecdotal comments around the photos. Dad always took the time that was needed to show my mother in concrete ways how much he loved her, and certainly his actions were paramount in keeping their love strong and fresh all through the years.

THESE PAGES | *Dad never ceased adoring my mother (top), writing her notes and letters and giving her cards (above and opposite).* FOLLOWING PAGES | *A final kiss always followed my parent's rousing performance of "Jackson."*

June 23 1994
Odense, Denmark,

Happy Birthday Princess,

We get old and get used to each other. We think alike. We read each others minds. We know what the other wants without asking. Sometimes we irritate each other a little bit. Maybe sometimes take each other for granted.

But once in awhile, like today, I meditate on it and realize how lucky I am to share my life with the greatest woman I ever met. You still fascinate and inspire me. You influence me for the better. You're the object of my desire, the #1 Earthly reason for my existence. I love you very much.

Happy Birthday Princess.

John

CHAPTER FIVE

THE HOUSE ON THE LAKE

T WAS A COLD WINTER DAY AND A POT OF CHILI—MY FATHER'S RECIPE—WAS SIMMER-ING ON THE STOVE. HE WALKED BY THE POT AND THREW A HANDFUL OF SELF-RISING CORNMEAL INTO IT, OR REALLY, HE THREW IT AT THE POT. MOST OF THE CORNMEAL DID

not make it into the pot but rather scattered all over the stove, and more than a little landed on the floor below. Dad's recipe for chili contained a few unusual ingredients, one of which was self-rising cornmeal. Later in life he stopped making the chili himself, but he always made sure to add his own special touches. His methods were not always grace-ful, however.

"Stir it up, Kti!" he said with a smile to the cook, who rolled her eyes at him in annoyance. She did stir, albeit not dutifully.

Dad was a great cook, in his own inimitable way. In addition to chili, he had a repertoire of home-style dishes, including fried chicken.

When I was young, my father and I would go to his farm in Bon Aqua in Hickman County, Tennessee. We would stop at the grocery on the way and stock up. Inset is a typical shopping list for those trips.

CRISCO—ONE TUB.
MARTHA WHITE CORNMEAL,
TWO-POUND BAG.
WHITE BREAD.
ONE DOZEN EGGS.
COUNTRY-STYLE SAUSAGE.
SELF-RISING FLOUR.
RAW PEANUTS.
FROZEN PIZZAS.
BOLOGNA.
TWO CANS OF BISCUITS.
BUTTERMILK
WHOLE MILK
ORANGE JUICE
LITTLE DEBBIE
SNACK CAKES

After we had carried the groceries and overnight bags into the farmhouse, Dad would grab his shotgun and we would take to the woods. Usually we came back with a rab-bit and a squirrel, plenty to eat for the two of us. Dad would clean our kill and put the cut-up pieces in saltwater to draw out the blood. Then he would roll the pieces in flour and salt and pepper and fry in Crisco until golden brown, always in a cast-iron skillet. After the game was fried up, he would make gravy out of the leftover grease and spoon this concoction on top of biscuits.

In the morning it was usually fried eggs, sausage, more biscuits, and gravy, this time sausage gravy.

Peanuts were for snacks, and Dad always roasted his own. He would grab a hunk of skin on his arm and pinch it as he chewed. "See that, son?" he would say, gesturing toward his arm. "See that? Peanuts. You are what you eat." Then he would laugh.

ABOVE | *A shopping list for one of the trips my dad and I used to take to his farm in Bon Aqua, Tennessee.*
OPPOSITE | *My parents' lakeside home at 200 Caudill Drive in Hendersonville, Tennessee, was a massive stone and wood structure of some fourteen thousand square feet with vaulted ceilings. It was like no other place on Earth.*

Bon Aqua Spring Oct. '87

It's good water
The spring at the back of the far...
I walked across the new cut hay fie...
Over the barbed wire fence
Down the slope through the
Red October dogwoods.
The sun had set when I reached
The tree lined slope.
But I knew the trail down to the spri...
In the deepening twilight
I turned on my flashlight,
Not to find my way,
But to search the path for
Another Arrowhead.
I had found several here
Over the past fifteen years.
But it hadn't rained lately
So there were none this time.
I knelt at the spring flowing out of the roc...
I cupped my hands seven times,
And drank seven times
(Just a little personal ritual of mine)
Walking back up the slope
I met a full moon rising
Such beauty

Lunch was fried bologna with white bread and mustard. Dinner, if it wasn't game or chili, was frozen pizzas. Not exactly a healthy diet, but this was the way the man ate when he was the one behind the stove.

Old Bon Aqua Iron Pot was what Dad called his chili. Sometimes he called it Black Bart, although I have no idea why. When he cooked it himself, it was an all-day affair. He would sweat over the stove for hours, chopping onions, his eyes watering. The steak was cut up in large chunks, the cans of beans scattered about the kitchen, and, of course, the cornmeal was all over the place. Now I make the same chili, which is mostly unchanged from Dad's original recipe. I would love to share it with you, but first, a little Cash family chili philosophy.

Chili is an art, and to master it you have to go beyond the recipe. The recipe below is not a formula; it's only a guide. Dad believed that even the best recipe should be adapted to the cook's taste. So sample your creation as you make it so that it suits your palate.

Although Mom was the better cook, Dad was not afraid to give it all he had, and his creativity showed in many ways. He was adept at frying foods, truly his favorite method of preparation. He made fried chicken, fried turkey breast strips, country-fried steak, fried catfish, and, of course, fried squirrel and rabbit.

When Dad got older, his love for fried foods and the like did not dwindle, but he was happy to let someone else do the frying. He grew accustomed to our Sunday visits and expected my wife, Laura, and I to bring fried chicken each time. We brought over the grandchildren and the fried chicken. If for some reason we could not make it, both my parents were sorely disappointed.

Dad liked his chicken extra crispy. First he would remove the fried skin off his portion and eat it. Only then would he try a bite or two of the chicken.

Dad's fried dishes were not the norm in our house when I was growing up. But there was always plenty of food. Some of my family's favorite dishes were tomato gravy with homemade biscuits, Mom's "stuff" (a combination of potatoes and other vegetables fried in a pan, and then finished off with hot pepper cheese), and "son of a bitchin' stew," which was my grandfather Ezra's creation. It contained various meats and vegetables—everything the icebox had to offer.

My parents were endlessly creative in the kitchen. During the 1990s, one of the family favorites was Cashburgers. In the box below is the recipe in Dad's own handwriting.

OPPOSITE | *Dad's farm in Bon Aqua, Tennessee, was always a place of prayer, relaxation, and solace for him.* BELOW | *The truth is my parents liked all kinds of good food. Here, in my father's own handwriting, is one of the healthier recipes—our family's own particular version of veggie burgers. Also included is a recipe for Dad's soya grit bread, which was always a hit. And there are directions for making his Black Bart chili. It took him thirty-seven attempts to perfect it.*

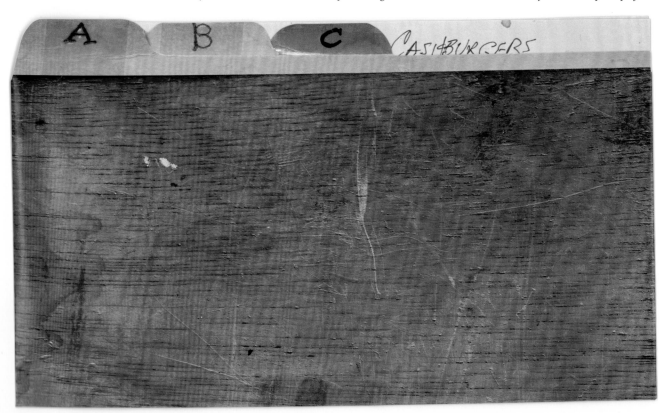

Although Dad enjoyed cooking at the farm in Bon Aqua, most of the cooking, living, and loving took place at the House on the Lake. It was home, the heart of my parents' lives. Dad stumbled on the house accidentally.

After leaving Vivian and moving to Tennessee, Dad had been living in Madison in an apartment not too far away from my mother's home. His roommate was Waylon Jennings. Since they both spent a lot of time on the road, they were able to give each other enough space. If they had been in such close quarters all the time, I doubt their friendship would have lasted. Dad told me that two men should never live together, that it would ruin their friendship. As far as I know, since Dad's time in the air force, Waylon was his one and only male roommate.

So in 1967 Dad went to find a place to call his own and discovered it at 200 Caudill Drive in Hendersonville, just north of Nashville. Dad bought the home from its builder, Braxton Dixon, in 1967 while on an excursion to investigate the lakeside lots in the area.

The story goes that Dad pulled up in his Cadillac and walked straight up to Braxton.

"Do you plan on this being your home?" he asked.

"It will be when I'm finished with it," Braxton responded.

Dad shook his head with a smile. "No, it will be my home," he responded.

"Sorry, but no," said Braxton.

Dad pulled out his checkbook. "Name the price," he said.

And so Braxton relented eventually and sold the property to my father, who also bought the surrounding one hundred and fifty acres.

I remember the home I lived in as a boy and teenager fondly. It was a welcoming place, with wide and tall windows and high ceilings (the master bedroom's was over twenty feet tall). All three floors were packed full of furniture, mostly Renaissance Revival pieces from the nineteenth century. My mother would brag that in all of their homes put together there were over eighty beds (though many of them were dismantled). There were a goodly few strewn throughout the House on the Lake.

When we weren't touring, summer brought lazy days spent swimming and cooking out. I can visualize the doorjamb where my height was notched as I grew. My father's height was also marked to show when I passed his six foot one inches at the age of fifteen. I remember the round bedroom that was mine, where I had set up a drum set on the wooden frame of the round bed in its center. My rock band would play loud music, my parents ever patient and always allowing us to crank it up.

I recall the quiet Sunday mornings, long before there was cable, sitting with my parents and reading the Bible, while our coonhound Molly curled up on the living room couch.

She was the only dog my mother ever allowed in any of her houses.

The House on the Lake was mostly a happy place. Dad loved to laugh; he had a great sense of humor. Though good friends with Elvis Presley, Dad often did a silly impersonation of him on his show during the 1950s. Elvis returned the compliment by imitating my father on some of his own live shows.

OPPOSITE TOP | *The photo on the left shows the House on the Lake during construction, likely in 1967. The photo on the right is the home as I knew it growing up, grand and magnificent.* OPPOSITE BOTTOM | *My father and mother at home with each other in the House on the Lake.* TOP | *Contrary to his public image, Dad had quite a sense of humor and was always clowning around.* ABOVE | *Dad also did a mean Elvis impersonation.*

Dad had friends who loved him dearly and wanted nothing from him but his friendship. They were producers, musicians, farmers, and businessmen. When I think of these easygoing relationships, the first person who comes to mind is "Cowboy" Jack Clement. Cowboy first met Dad at Sun Records in 1956. He was the original engineer on many of Dad's early recordings and also penned a few of Dad's early hits.

Dad laughed and told jokes with Cowboy and sometimes was just plain silly. I remember seeing Dad at the Cowboy Arms Hotel and Recording Spa dressed in a top hat, with a child's pig-nose disguise around his face. He was carrying a small amplifier on a shoulder strap while playing guitar. Cowboy would join in and they would dance around the studio.

DAD HAD FRIENDS WHO LOVED HIM DEARLY AND WANTED NOTHING FROM HIM BUT HIS FRIENDSHIP.

Other dear friends at the "spa" were David Ferguson (Dad's long-time engineer), Chance Martin, and Jim Varney. There were a host of others, too many to mention, who also frequented the studio.

Times were fun during the 1980s for Dad, especially from 1984 on. He made a lot of great music at Cowboy's studio during that period. Although Dad was dropped by Columbia in 1986, he didn't let this stifle his creativity. Some have argued that the eighties were a low point, but Dad did some great work with Cowboy, including the album *Water from the Wells of Home*, which consisted of duets with everyone from Paul McCartney to Roy Acuff.

Each Christmas we would have parties, and family and friends would come from around the country, or the world

---

ABOVE | *My parents hosted many memorable meals for friends from around the world and all walks of life. Here (left to right) are Dad, U2's Adam Clayton, Doug Caldwell, "Cowboy" Jack Clement, and U2's Bono enjoying a delicious Southern-style lunch.*

sometimes, to join us. At the time Mom's daughter Carlene was married to rocker Nick Lowe, and the couple lived in England. Nick would bring his bandmates and friends. Other holiday season visitors included Elvis Costello, Tom Petty, the Heartbreakers, and Bono and Adam Clayton from U2.

When I left home at the age of eighteen, I was certain that I was my own man and unaware that I was not done growing up. I saw my mother cry as I walked out the door, my belongings in my arms as I headed for my first apartment. I remember Mom and Dad both saying "You always have a place at home, son," their eyes sad but strong.

But later, when I was lost, I remember trying to go back and finding that the novelist Thomas Wolfe was correct: You can never go home again. Nevertheless, through the years that house was a beacon. I created another home eventually, but I truly believe that in our heart of hearts, our family home is our true home. I will always remember it that way.

After my parents passed, the family estate sold the house and lakeside lot to Barry Gibb of the Bee Gees. It was in great need of some work to restore it to its original splendor, and Barry and his wife, Linda, renovated the house. After months of work, the place was two weeks away from moving day.

On April 10, 2007, I was in Oregon with my wife and family. I was driving across the Yaquina Bay Bridge in Newport when my phone rang. It was the entertainer and musician Marty Stuart, a longtime friend of my father's who at one time had been married to my sister Cindy.

When I answered, I heard the desperation in Marty's voice. "It's burning down, John Carter," he said. I felt a chill as I pulled over to the side of the road beyond the bridge. "I'm watching it burn to the ground. They are trying to put the fire out, but it's too far gone."

I sat and cried on the phone with Marty that day. Losing that house was for me like losing a loved one. Its demise signaled the passing of an age. The House on the Lake had been destined to be home to only one family: the Cashes.

ABOVE | *This is a photograph of the ruin of the House on the Lake as it stands at the time of this publication. When I heard about the house burning, it felt to me like someone had died, and I grieved for quite some time.* FOLLOWING PAGES | *A "guitar pull" in the lakeside room at the House on the Lake. Here, Dad, Kris Kristofferson (second from right), and Chris Gantry (second from left) listen to one of Shel Silverstein's most assuredly rousing performances.*

CHAPTER SIX

RAINBOW-COLORED GLASSES

AD WAS A HUGE FAN OF THE PAINTER AND SCULPTOR FREDERIC REMINGTON AND HAD A FEW ORIGINAL CASTINGS OF HIS BRONZES, PLUS A SKETCHBOOK OF HIS DOODLES. BUT DAD'S STYLE WAS NOT INFLUENCED IN THE LEAST BY REMINGTON, OR ANY OTHER

painter. Art was not something that Dad studied, and he never attempted to copy any technique. He probably could not have told you whether his style was inspired by surrealism, or abstract expressionism, or any other art movement. Instead, art was a very personal therapy to him, something he cherished, but not as most artists do. It was almost as if each work he painted was in some way simply an extension of his signature. Much of it resembled lines and colors splashed across a white canvas. But it is undeniable that he expressed his emotions and state of mind in this art. From the first time I saw my dad's drawings and paintings, I have been enthralled.

My dad's lifelong love of sketching and doodling began at an early age. His humor and unique sense of irony are evident in these drawings.

In the early 1990s, Dad's jaw was broken when a bone shattered during a particularly intense dental surgery. There was massive nerve damage, and he was in horrific agony. A bone graft was done, and his jaw was wired shut, forcing Dad to cancel his tours for an extended period. During the prolonged recovery, a doctor suggested he purchase a writing pad and pastels and put his pains down on the page. I am not sure if this helped relieve the pain itself, but it certainly gave him a release.

Art was therapy to him. Even at the end of his life, he used the pen as a form of self-expression, a way to put his suffering and pains on paper.

Throughout his life, my father always had a tremor in his hand, which was noticeable in his handwriting and also his art. But he used it to his advantage, adding dynamic intensity to his style. His Christian

---

THESE PAGES | *To my father, art had no restrictions. He was a true "American Primitive."*
He greatly enjoyed sketching and photography, carrying a camera with him whenever he could.

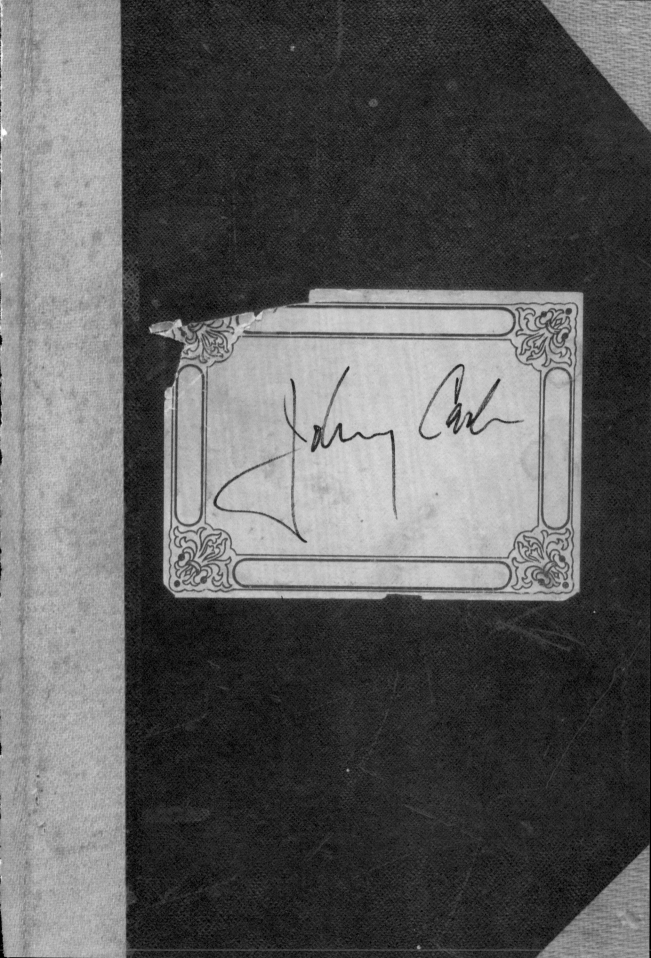

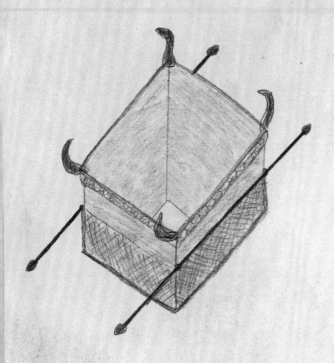

Illustration #1.

outer Court, Fence & Gate.

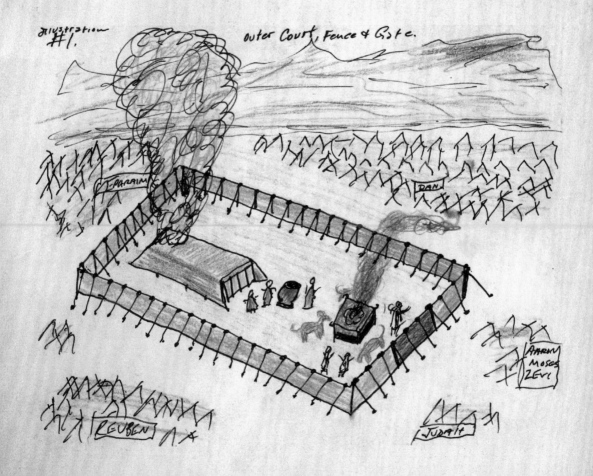

EPHRAIM

DAN

AARON
MOSES
LEVI

REUBEN

JUDAH

OPPOSITE | *These three sketches of Biblical themes were done while Dad was studying to become an ordained minister. Top left: The Brazen Altar. Top right: The Lauer. Bottom: Outer Court, Fence and Gate.* THIS PAGE | The Shroud, *Dad's charcoal sketch of the mysterious Shroud of Turin, which supposedly shows the face of Christ.*

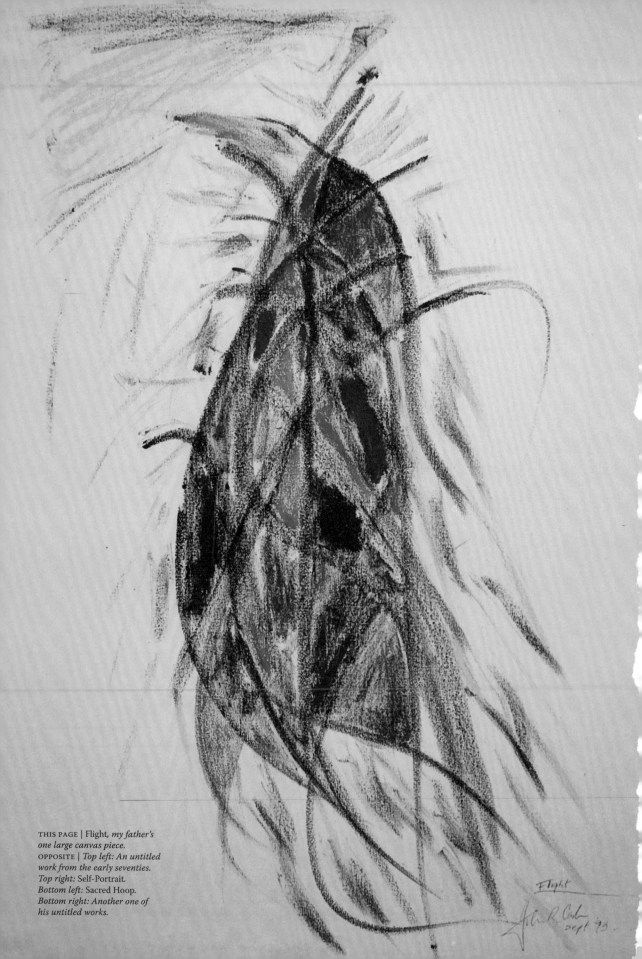

THIS PAGE | Flight, *my father's one large canvas piece.*
OPPOSITE | *Top left: An untitled work from the early seventies.*
Top right: Self-Portrait.
Bottom left: Sacred Hoop.
Bottom right: Another one of his untitled works.

Flight

J.R. Cash
5-25-73

Johnny Cash
Self Portrait
March 18 1991

Sacred Hoop
of the Cycle
April 14
1991

J.R. Cash
June 26 '73

YES, IT SEEMS
THAT LIFE
CAN BE COLOR-
FUL IF WE ALLOW
IT TO BE.

JRC

studies led him to pull out charcoal or pen and express his excitement about his faith in works such as *Armageddon*, a dark and foreboding vision of the apocalypse, and *The Shroud*, a charcoal representation of the supposed face of Christ, drawn from the Shroud of Turin.

Dad painted not to prove anything but to express himself. There were those who supported Dad's art, the aforementioned doctor being one. And I certainly must express gratitude to Dad's dear friend Bill Miller for his encouragement of my father. It was Bill who suggested he paint his only work that we have on a large canvas, which is called *Flight*.

I remember Dad drawing, his pastel pencils out, making his scribbles and streaks chaotically across the pages. He would slash five or six brush strokes across the easel and then glare at his work, attempting to decipher it. More often than not, he would wad the paper up and throw it in the trash. Sometimes he would set the painting in a stack and move on to the next.

My father had a Leicaflex camera, and during the 1970s, he was a prolific photographer. Chance Martin, an employee of my father's at the time, remembers Dad buying this camera in Germany in 1976. According to Chance, what got Dad interested in photography was a fan book that Chance had put together for Dad. Chance, a photographer himself, had published a few of his own photos in this book, which was sold on the road show as a souvenir.

He introduced Dad to macro-photography on a two-week trip to my family's vacation home in Jamaica, Cinnamon Hill Great House. With a macrolens, a photographer can take very close-up shots of tiny subjects, which look huge in the final shot. Dad took a great many photos on this trip to Jamaica with Chance at his side. He photographed every small object he could get close to—skulls, bats, scorpions, and flowers. Despite his tremor, Dad held a steady hand for these shots. He also took many great photos of landscapes and, of course, of people—people he loved and those he found intriguing. He had a way of seeing the story in their eyes and capturing it with his camera. Dad had a photographer's magical eye. He mostly used only natural light, adjusting his camera's aperture as necessary.

It was a sight to see when Dad was on one of his shoots. He sometimes would go out from a hotel, whether it was in a small European town or in New York City, his camera around his neck and his bag over his shoulder. I would follow.

One day when we were in London, walking through Piccadilly Circus, we stopped so that he could take some shots of architecture.

"My goodness," called a lady who watched the photographer beside me. "Are you Johnny Cash?"

Dad put the camera down and smiled back at her.

"Why, yes, Mum, I am," he said.

The lady fumbled in her purse for her camera. By the time she raised it, Dad had beaten her to the punch, holding up his own and snapping a shot of her before she could get him.

He laughed and we both posed for her photo.

OPPOSITE | *To Dad, art was fun and a release, but it was also much more: Quite often, it was an important form of therapy.* ABOVE | *Most people remember my father clad in black. I remember him wearing this somewhat ragged bush jacket, its pockets usually stuffed with 35mm film canisters, pens, and foldout maps.*

TOP | *My father's photograph of the church above held special meaning for him. It is located near Kingsland, Arkansas, where he was born.* ABOVE | *Dad was especially fond of macrophotography, often turning his lens to flowers.* OPPOSITE | *A photograph my father took of the fields of Megiddo in the Holy Land, one of two photographs he titled* Armageddon.

OPPOSITE | *Dad took this photo in the Holy Land in 1977. Here the tour group, comprising the whole Johnny Cash Show band, crew, and a good many family members, board the bus idling on the road to Masada, Israel. My parents sold their Rolls Royce limousine to fund the trip for everyone.* ABOVE | *Dad's photography focused frequently on landscapes, both breathtaking (top) and more mundane (above), beautifully capturing light.*

OPPOSITE | *The four photos on the left were taken from the window in Dad's office at the House on the Lake during the four key seasons of the year: spring, summer, fall, and winter.* TOP | *This is the second of Dad's* Armageddon *images from the Holy Land.* ABOVE | *These are two other great examples of his mac-rophotography.*

97

THESE PAGES | *Some of Dad's best photographs are of people, nature, and animals. That's a young me playing with a frog in the front yard at Cinnamon Hill, Jamaica.*

CHAPTER SEVEN

FROM HEART TO PEN

DAD'S THOUGHTS AND WORDS SEEMED TO TAKE THE MOST DIRECT ROUTE FROM HIS HEART TO PEN AND PAPER. HE HAD A SIMPLE, HONEST STYLE THAT NONE COULD MATCH. HE WAS AMAZINGLY PROLIFIC, TOO, AND WROTE THROUGHOUT HIS LIFE. WHEN THINGS

were good, he wrote. When he was struggling—whether with physical pain, relationship issues, or addiction—he wrote. When he was alone and searching for the inner peace he needed, he wrote. Pen and paper were his constant companions all the days of his life.

Dad knew what he wanted to do with his life most certainly when he returned from the air force. He was determined to pursue music, although perhaps this was not a choice. Maybe the music simply had to come out. Perhaps his poetry and songs were his very lifeblood, somehow predestined to emerge during his lifetime and lead his spirit onward.

Dad was endlessly creative and energetic, always pursuing a fresh idea for a song that caught his heart. Of course, he will be most remembered by his most famous

compositions, including "Folsom Prison Blues," "I Walk the Line," and "Hey Porter," to name a few. But it is the creative process that intrigues me the most. A man like my father is remembered by his successes and not by his failures, and he had a great deal of both. But even the fragments of his unfinished works can give one insight into his unique method of creativity.

Dad found inspiration for his music easily. Much of his writing was introspective. In "I Walk the Line," for example, he examined his dedication to his mate. He revised his songs a great deal, but more often than not, his initial from-the-gut concept was what he settled with in the end.

To my father, poetry—like painting and photography—was an avenue for free self-expression. He held to no rule or principle, except to let the ink flow. His spirit controlled the process completely.

ABOVE | *My father never ceased writing songs and poetry.*
OPPOSITE | *My father in the studio in late 1959, pen in his shirt pocket.*

Death and Hell

Death and hell are never full
And neither are the eyes of men
Cats can fly
From nine stories high
And pigs can see the wind

She stepped down from her carriage at 10 vermillion St
I took off my roustabout and laid it at her feet
She took me in her parlour and she cooled me with her fan
But said I'll go no further with a music making man
I said lady I'll be good if you will let me stay
Just a drink from wisdoms well and I'll be on my way
She laughed and heaven filled the room, said this I give to you
~~This body knows no wisdom~~, but ~~this I give too~~
This bodys wisdom is the flesh heres a thing or two
She let me make my pallet ~~in~~ the moonlight on the floor
Just outside of ~~paradise~~ but in hells back door
The image of her nibbled at the edges of my soul
My ~~dreams were~~ a hurricane and quite out of control
But I awoke to ~~sucking gargoyles~~ lavender and ~~red~~
the ~~second station of the cross was just above my head~~
I awoke to gargoyles and a hard bench for my bed
The second station of the cross was just above my head
~~Her sweet voice came to the dream and she said troubadour~~
Then came her voice thru the storm, its in the flesh a deal
~~You should know youd have to pay for wisdom that you~~
You know you'll have to pay for wisdom that you try to steal

On the facing page is a song my father and I wrote together. It had an unusual source of inspiration for sure. We were traveling on the bus between shows during a series of one-night stands. Dad read in the newspaper a very unusual scientific study: It had been determined that when a cat fell from a window three to nine stories high, it would normally die upon landing because its body was tense and the cat felt the full impact of the fall. However, if the cat fell out of a window more than nine stories high, it had enough time to stretch out and relax its limbs and torso, which helped it survive. We laughed about this all day. Dad had also read somewhere that according to an old wives' tale, pigs can see the wind. Inspired by these two unique bits of information, we developed the chorus for the song "Death and Hell." The main story came from our imaginations. It was recorded on the Highwaymen album *The Road Goes on Forever*.

HE HELD TO NO RULE OR PRINCIPLE, EXCEPT TO LET THE **INK FLOW.**

One song that comes to mind when talking about my dad's creative process is "The Man Comes Around," which appears on the album *American IV*. I recall the first day Dad showed me the song. The concept for the song had come to him in a dream, a very unusual one. In his dream he entered Queen Elizabeth's court and humbly approached the throne. She looked up at him and said, "You're like a thorn tree in a whirlwind."

He awoke wondering what this could mean and began to study the Scriptures, certain that he would find the solution there. This began the process of writing the song that is arguably one of the greatest compositions of his later life.

Dad called me and asked that I come to his office and hear a new song. I arrived and after a short visit with my mother, went to see Dad. He was sitting at his desk, and there on his table were at least twenty sheets. Some of the papers were just short fragments

OPPOSITE | *A draft of "Death and Hell," a song Dad and I wrote together in 1993.* ABOVE | *My father on the front porch of the house he grew up in, in Dyess, Arkansas.*

But the music never stops.
It's an unending loop
through my brain, over
and over and over again.
    Finally my head settles
on that one particular
song and won't let go.
    I wrote and recorded
" The man comes Around early
on in this project, and for
three or four months I
re-cycled that song over
and over until I'd have
to get up out of bed

The Man Comes Around

Spoken
You can be first on the draw
You can kill your mother in law
You can steal some pilgrims Mackinaw
But you gotta know it'll be written down
When the man comes around —

V. 1.
Theres a man going 'round taking names
And decides who to free and who to blame
Everybody wont be treated all the same
There'll be a golden ladder coming down
When the man comes around

V. 2
The hairs on your head will stand up
When all you're trying to do is stand up
Will you partake of that last offered cup
Or disappear into the potters ground
When the man comes around.

1st Chorus
You will hear ten million trumpets
Ten million angels will be singing
Multitudes are marching
To the big kettle Drum
Somewhere there are voices crying
Some are borning some are dying
Alpha and Omega's
On the day of Kingdom Come

OPPOSITE AND ABOVE | *My father's music kept coming and coming throughout his life. When he was working on a song he truly loved, he would spend a lot of time with it and sometimes rewrite verses and create alternate versions. Opposite is a note he wrote explaining his heartfelt obsession with his composition, "The Man Comes Around." Above is one of the many variations of the lyrics he drafted for this song.*

of lyrics, and some were longer versions, but they were all various notations and versions of "The Man Comes Around."

Dad picked up his guitar. "Hey, thanks for coming by so soon. I want to play you this new song," he said eagerly. The excitement in his voice was clear.

And so he began to strum and sing the song. As I remember, it was note for note and lyrically exactly the version we wound up with as the final recording.

"Wow, Dad," I said as he finished. "That is unbelievable. I love the part about 'virgins trimming their wicks.'"

His eyes lit up again. He reached and picked up his Bible. It was always on his desk. "Let me show you. That is a parable of sorts. Aren't you familiar with it?" I had to admit I wasn't. He showed me the Scripture, opening to the twenty-fifth chapter of Matthew. As he read out loud, I looked more closely at the sheets of paper on his desk. There were a good few additional verses.

When he finished reading, I asked him what those

> "WHEN I GET ONTO A GOOD THING... I JUST KEEP WRITING."

pages were. "Oh, when I get onto a good thing that I'm excited about, I just keep writing. Those are various versions that I may include in the song."

Later, while recording, Dad did try a few of these verses. But the original version was the strongest. The exciting burst of inspiration that resulted in this song was so important to him.

Dad had asthma and battled it through the last few years of his life. But his persistence and ability to laugh at his own mortality stayed with him. Dad was in and out of the hospital with pneumonia quite often the last year of his life. Not two months before he died, he began to work on "Like the 309," a song that shows perseverance and humor in the face of death, and which can be heard on *American V.*

Through each and every stage of his life, the man always wrote and made music. It was his career but also his life's therapy, his very breath and blood. Though life doled out pain and suffering, loss and solitude, his creativity endured.

ABOVE | *Dad studying the lyrics to the Depeche Mode song "Personal Jesus" in Rick Rubin's studio. To Dad, the song was a statement about his personal salvation.*
OPPOSITE | *My father never failed to stop and appreciate the beauty of nature and the wonders therein.*

Autumn

Even now
the red and golden leaves
Are burning up the hills
And winter will come ~~soon~~
The leaves will turn dark
As the snow begins to cover them
But the earth beneath
Will be warm
Holding the promised renewal
Of spring.
Then the green shoots
Of grass, flowers, weeds and herbs
Will burst thru the birdsong days
Of spring.
And as it has done for eons past
The glory of growth,
Flowering and fruits
Will ~~illuminate~~ the land
Then as harvest falls
The red and golden leaves
Will burn up the hills
And I would walk in awe
and wonder
And thankfulness
To again witness
This miracle

Oct. 87
JR

You wonder how ~~where~~ true love goes
No one can say - cause nobody knows
Like rain on a rock - Like a leaf in the air
No way to tell - But its going somewhere
You wonder what - True love knows
No one can say - Cause nobody knows.
It dont make sense - Like a midnite sun
And one and one - is only one

Heart on heart - and soul on soul
Body on Body   is how it goes
Heart on heart and soul on soul
Body on body - is all it knows.

I woke up this morning
And I looked into the mirror
And I saw lines I hadn't seen before
But I smiled back at the image
Of a walking talking miracle
Who's lived a dozen lifetimes, Maybe More
So I found my book of numbers
And I called my inner circle
Of ones who have so long been tried and true
I said lets get together now
Cause I have really missed you
It's been way too long since I saw you

Just a few good friends

ABOVE | *Most of Dad's poems are short or unfinished fragments, but all of them demonstrate true heart and spirit and a strong capacity for love and self-reflection.* OPPOSITE | *Dad in the studio in late 1959, shortly after the move to Columbia Records in 1958.*

you tell me that I must Perish
Like the flowers that I cherish
Nothing remaining of my name
Nothing remembered of my fame
But the trees that I planted
~~Sti~~ still are young

The Songs I sang
Will still be sung

End
I have scars upon my arms
That show how I have lived
I've a slight limp in my walk
To tell you I once fell
I've forgiveness in my heart
Both given and received.
I've a promis in my heart
That I wont go to hell

OPPOSITE | *Friends join Dad in the studio during the same recording session documented in the photos on the preceding page.* ABOVE | *My father always believed in the life eternal and often wrote poetry to express his faith and hope.*

Don't Take your Guns

① A young cowboy named Billy Joe
                    (Ten years old)
   Billy Joe sits on front steps playing
with dog, throwing rocks at can,
shooting slingshot, whittling, etc.
                    Fade
   B. Joe comes out of house with boots
on, hat in hand, gun belt on, Colt
45 hangs to ankle.
   B.J.'s mother (Ten year old girl with
grey wig on follows him, hands out,
pleading:
Don't take your guns to town son
Leave your   "   "   at home Bill
   "   "   "   "   "   "   "

2. "He laughed and kissed his mom and said
   your B.J.'s a man"
       B.J. kisses mom on cheek.
       She grimaces
   I can shoot as quick and straight
   As anybody can
       B.J. takes out gun, tries to
           twirl it, cant.
   "But I wouldn't shoot without
   a cause, I'd gun nobody down"
   B.J. Puts gun in holster, puts on hat
           turns to go.
   "But his mother cried as he walked out
       Don't take your guns to town son
       Leave your guns at home Bill
       "   "   "   "   "   "
   Mother pleads dramatically then gets
       firm, shakes her finger at him

OPPOSITE | *My father's handwritten treatment for a music video for his song "Don't Take Your Guns to Town." He would often write for his television show and wrote a screenplay (*Gospel Road*), two autobiographies (*Man in Black *and *Cash: The Autobiography*), and a novel (*Man in White*).* ABOVE | *Dad playing one of his favorite guitars in front of the fireplace in the lakeside room at the House on the Lake.*

ABOVE | *Mom lovingly watches Dad. She always saw the light and goodness in every situation.* OPPOSITE | *Although my parents traveled the globe for most of their lives, it was home that always meant the most to them—not a building of stone and wood, but the family that resided within.*

For June
With All my Love
John

A Little Patch of Grass
by J.R. Cash Sept. '82

In a world of cold concrete and steel
And tinted window panes
I walked the streets among the clones
With man made programmed brains
The subway rumbled at my feet
The bums, the sick, the old
I said that never, ever could
Life such as this be whole
I met a bright eyed beauty
Had she fallen from the sun?
I smiled and she returned it
Then she crossed on Green to run
I quickly made the other side
And followed just behind
Haltingly I said to her
Lady, please, if you dont mind:

    I saw it in your smile
    And your eyes just as we passed
    Like me, I think you'd leave it all
    For a little patch of grass
    I'd take you across a rippling stream
    We'd hear the shallow water laugh,
    As hand in hand we wade toward
    A little patch of grass

We could lie upon our backs
And smile up at the sky
A million miles from everything
Where nothing rushes by
She looked around the city
Then she looked me up and down
Are you for real? she asked me
I said yes, but not this town
We walked and talked of common things
Then: "I dont even know your name
I said, whats the difference
When our hearts cry for the same

Johnny Cash

Dec 31 1976
Cinnamon Hill.

This has been my best year yet in many ways. Family-wise, it's all been beautiful. We are close. I guess I love June Carter more than ever. There's a kind of a bond between us; an understanding that is a precious thing.

I can see that she is a better person, a stronger Christian than ever, and I'm sure a lot of it has to do with the daily hours she spends in her bible.

I guess I test her and try her quite often, 'cause quite often I cause a pained look on her face by my lack of patience, unkindliness (and irritableness) She always turns love with whatever I give her and I'm still learning many lessons from her. My shortcoming is failing to reply in kind.

John Carter started to school in Sept, and he's been sheer joy. I love that 5 am alarm clock, when I can get up, and fix the coffee build a fire and help get him ready for school. I enjoy every minute of that ten-mile drive with him to Goodpasture school.

In this area I think I have not failed. No father spends the time with a son than I do John Carter. We took those fishing trips I promised on Labor day 1974. I took him back to his roots in Arkansas, and I think he learned and loved the lesson of his Cash heritage. — Then there was the Carter family homecoming in Virginia. He explored his Carter heritage and understood his roots there, and loved every minute of it.

My relationship with him is a solid bond of love, and he knows it, as I do. We give him everything his heart desires, and we may pay for it, but I can't help it.

Prospects for 1969

1. My own Summer TV Show
2. " " Fall TV Show
3. Host Kraft Music Hall
4 Movies
5.

page 5 1968
⑥ Dec. 1968 New york Kraft Music
Hall

Tragedies:

⑦ Luthers death - The fire - the
intensive care unit. - dead - funeral.
Marshall Fluke Roy Margie Gressett
etc - -

⑧ Sept 1968 - Bob Wootton "accidental"
discovery - Fayetteville Ark. Gov
Rockefeller

⑨ 1968 Nov Jimmy Howard death.
Jan - Corky Harlan Waylon June
& Jan - Military funeral

31st
9:10 Pm

Fishing in Old Hickory - Looking for arrowheads with Braxton - Garden - Best Garden ever - New evergreen trees Jim & Pop Carter - Pool finished - Garage -

(4) (Show dates $4000 to $12000 this year) (per day)

Roy Orbisons house Burns - I acquire his lot, plan orchard. Buy property near Smithville with Braxton -

(5) Oct 1968 DJ Convention CMA Show "Folsom" top Album - Nominated for top entertainer. - [Glen Campbell TV show] Carnegie Hall (sellout - Standing ovation) Palladium (sellout - Standing ovation) ditto every English date

(6) Filming of documentary - Wounded Knee S.D. - Medicine Men - "Big foot" - Show at St. Francis - turn away crowd - Tennessee State Prison

Page 3 1968
3 May 1968 England Scotland +
Albert Hall - Front page Glasgow
Good reviews. —
   Israel - praying - getting recorder -
Valley of David - Jerusalem - King
David Hotel - Via Dolorosa - Calvary
— Emotional experience - Jacob - Beth-
Lehem - Dead Sea - (taste of water)
Qumran - Jericho — refugee tents
+ huts - Gethsemane — Mt of Olives
Wailing Wall - Haifa - (the view from
the hotel) - Cesarea - Nazareth —
Cana - Tiberias - Sea of Galilee
Beduins - Magdala - Mt of Beautitudes
— St Peters perch — Mt Tabor —
Valley of Jezrael — Haifa - Cesarea-
Tel Aviv - Dan Hotel + Israeli food
(Bacon + Eggs - Show + Dinner with CBS
Water skiing with six girls

Page 2, 1968.
Coach Kelley - My dad watching
the prisoners, tears in his eyes -
the warden giving me 12 cups. -
Leaving the prison - not too excited
about a possible album - Compliments
from everyone - Hugh Cherry - Bob
Johnston - Gene Beley - Robt Hilburn.
- - - - The later excitement over
the sound -

② My marriage to June Carter on March
1st 1968. A beautiful day in Franklin,
Ky. - Micky & Monroe - Luther
Margie Marshall, Etta Fluke Joyce
Kilgore - the church the audience
June Rosie Carlene crying - George
Morgan singing.

    The reception - People people people
Roger - Luther Alone with June.
Beautiful night.

HOUSE OF CASH

CAUDILL DRIVE
HENDERSONVILLE,
TENNESSEE 37075

Dec. 31ˢᵗ 1968
8:35 PM

To Myself.

I feel that this year, 1968 has been, in many ways, the best year of my 36 years of life.

It has been a sober, serious year. Also probably the busiest year of my life, as well as the most fulfilling.

Remembering back; without re-viewing dates and schedules — the first; high point this year was;

①. Feb. 1968 at Folsom Prison. June-My dad, Rev. Gressett, the Statlers, Carl Perkins. — the new song by the prisoner.— Rehearsal in the Sacremento Motel.— Luther, Marshall. Fluke.— The Show — Glen Sherley—

OPPOSITE | *For many years, Dad would write himself a letter on December 31, summarizing the year's events and looking to the next. These letters functioned like a personal inventory of sorts. In the one Dad wrote to himself at the end of 1968, he recounts one of the most important years of his life. It was important in so many ways: 1968 was the year of the Folsom Prison concert and the year he married my mother, among many other significant occurrences.* ABOVE | *Dad committed his whole being to his music and spent his whole life searching for inspiration and understanding.*

CHAPTER EIGHT

A STANDARD OF COMPARISON

DAD LEARNED HIS GREAT LOVE OF THE SEA FROM MY GRANDFATHER EZRA CARTER. OUR HOME IN PORT RICHEY, FLORIDA, JUST NORTH OF TAMPA, HAD BELONGED TO MAYBELLE AND EZRA FROM THE MID-SIXTIES UNTIL THEIR DEATHS IN THE

seventies. (This spacious home stayed in the family until 2002.) My grandfather was unafraid of the ocean and had once been stranded out in the ocean for two days. His boat was only a fifteen-foot skiff. The tale goes that when the Coast Guard found him, alone and washed out who knows how far from shore, he had his fishing pole in hand, and he was laughing and still trying to fill his cooler with fish. I was fascinated by his hearty nature and wanted to be just like him. As it turned out, Dad and I would have our own adventure.

There was a citrus orchard in the backyard of our Florida home, which Dad took great pleasure in, pruning the trees and reaping the harvest every summer. We were there a lot. He loved the weather and the sun. We had friends, the Littles, who had a house built on stilts in the shallow ocean just beyond the

Pithlachascotee River channel. Our home was on the Cotee, as the locals called it. Dad had numerous guests come stay with us there, including Billy and Ruth Graham. The friends, the orchard, and the sun were great, but our place in Florida was about one thing, really: fishing. We fished all the time. We set out chum lines for sharks and mackerel, but mostly we just went bottom fishing.

This story, as I remember it, is 100 percent true. We were sitting on the bridge of our twenty-five-foot not-quite-seaworthy boat and headed out into the great Gulf of Mexico, as we had every day that week. I was twelve that summer of 1982. Like my granddad, my father had no fear of the sea. We would go thirty or forty miles out, with no view of land in sight and with nothing but a two-way radio, which worked sometimes and at other times did not.

THESE PAGES | *I spent the first twenty-seven years of my life on tour with my parents, taking to the stage with them during almost every show. Above, my father reaches down to share the microphone with a young me. On the right, I help Dad tune his guitar onstage at the Carter Fold in Hiltons, Virginia. This was his second to last public performance, mere weeks before his passing.*

At Home - 8 PM.
Dec 31st 1972

Dear Reader,

I just read those letters I wrote on this day for the past four years and I must say!

John Cash you are going to slow down as of now! Those letters are shallow sketches of fast, irratic, mindless, ~~████~~, thoughtless rambling.

Yes congratulations John Cash on your superstardom! Big deal.

True, you must be grateful for Gods showers of blessings, but regardless of all you have been quoted as saying to the contrary, you are too excited ~~by~~ over your personal wealth, career successes and other vain fleeting things.

OK.

I hereby resolve, asking Gods help, that I shall court wisdom more and more in this my 41st year. Especially heavenly wisdom.

Its a quiet night here in the bedroom at home. June and John Carter went to sleep early, tired out. John Carter went to Paul Dahlhausers birthday party. Rosie has gone to Julie Morrow. And I am awake alone in this big house where love still lives thank God. That is the most important earthly thing. Peace at Home. Trust. Understanding, tolerance. Love!

That day we were heading out into the Gulf, its waters completely still. There wasn't a cloud in the sky. We had heard a report that some scattered thunderstorms might arrive in the afternoon, but we were used to that. In the great expanse of the ocean, we could pick out the storms on the horizon and avert them. Or at least this had worked before.

The fishing was good that day and we pulled in a diverse bounty. I was amazed at the variety of life to be found in the warm waters of the Gulf. We caught grunts, lips, black bass, snakefish, sand sharks, sand dabbers, dogfish, triggerfish, blowfish, tilefish, hogfish, and, of course, grouper, which, of all these, was the fish we wanted most. Things were different back then, and if there were limits on what or how much we could catch, we were unaware of them. We kept everything, putting live fish in the holding tank of the boat, where fresh water poured through all day, keeping them alive or at least fresh.

The day wore on and we kept fishing. We were not anchored and floated around with the motor turned off, bottom

fishing. This method was quite successful back then—there were many fish. We would go for a while and not get a bite, and then suddenly for fifteen minutes, we were catching fish after fish. Lots of fun, just a man and his son, forty miles out, no GPS or cell phone. And that was one of those days when the radio wasn't working.

I noticed a cloud on the horizon, thick, black, and dangerous looking, but far away. I looked at Dad and saw that he was looking at the same cloud.

"Well, son," he said, beginning to reel in his rod, "I s'pose we had best be heading back in."

I looked out toward the end of my rod and saw that there was, unbelievably, a small yellow bird on the tip.

"Look, Dad!" I cried. "Look at the little bird!"

He looked and smiled. "I guess we have a visitor, son. A finch. Wonder what he's doing so far out here?"

"I just don't know," I said, holding my rod tightly so as not to jerk the bird about. "Do you think he'll stay with us all the way back?" I asked.

OPPOSITE | *In some New Year's letters to himself, my father would look back over his life and actions and make searching self-appraisals. He was not afraid to admit he had been egotistical or self-righteous and did just that in the annual letter from 1972.* ABOVE | *From an early age, and throughout his life, my father was my absolute best friend.*

IN THE SPRING OF 1975

THE CARPENTERS WERE RE-
MODELING A BATHROOM IN THE
HOUSE RECENTLY. THEY
PULLED A BASEBOARD OFF AND
THERE WAS A BLACK SOCK,
OF MINE TIED IN A KNOT.
AND IN THE SOCK WERE ABOUT
500 BENNIES.

JOHN CARTER AND I WALKED
BY, AND THE CARPENTER PITCHED
THE SOCK TO ME, SAYING, "I'VE
FOUND THE FAMILY TREASURE,
MR CASH. I DON'T KNOW WHAT
THIS IS, BUT IT MUST BE YOURS."

I UNTIED THE SOCK AND
POURED THEM OUT IN MY
HAND; THE 20 MILLIGRAM WHITE
ONES WITH A CROSS ON THEM.

"WHAT IS IT DADDY," ASKED
JOHN CARTER

"POISON SON," I SAID. "LETS
FLUSH THEM."

AND WE DID.

Dad smiled. "Maybe so," he answered. "Now you best pull in your line." The wind had picked up in the past few minutes, causing the previously tranquil sea to ripple and rise in small swells. I felt a gusting breeze rise to my face, my hair blowing.

"Well, okay," I said and began to crank up the reel.

To my surprise the little bird stayed on the tip of my pole. Dad went over to the cockpit to start the boat, but when he turned the key, there was no sound at all.

"Well, what on earth?" he said, trying again, but still getting no response from the motor.

When I pulled in my line and set my rod down, the bird flew up and disappeared.

"What's wrong, Dad?"

"I just don't know, son. I just don't know."

My father was no mechanic. He could not tell you the difference between a radiator and a carburetor. He just had no understanding of machinery at all.

The wind was blowing strong now. "Well," he said reluctantly, "I guess I had better take a look."

And so he went back and opened the engine well, lay down on his stomach, and looked down into the oily compartment below, puzzled. I was on my knees beside him. I thought I smelled smoke. "Well, son, looks like we are just going to have to fix it ourselves," he said, but his tone betrayed the uncertainty he felt.

He got down in the belly of that boat and dug around in the darkness with just a penlight. He had a brand-new wrench, never before used, and with it he tightened the battery cables and knocked lightly on the spark plugs, trying everything his limited knowledge suggested.

"Son!" he called from the depths of the boat. "Son, try to start the engine!"

The wind was blowing hard now, and the boat was rocking steadily.

I turned the key, but still the engine made no sound.

"Nothing, Dad!" I cried.

"Well, dag-gum it!" he called in response.

Something caught my eye. I saw the little yellow bird again, now roosting on the starboard gunwales, close to the bow.

"Dad, the little bird is back," I called.

"Yes, he's most surely here to help," he answered.

I went back to the engine well and looked down. I could see my dad's posterior sticking out of a corner of the motor,

OPPOSITE | *It's well known that my father struggled with drugs throughout his life. Growing up with him, there were good times and bad, though the good always outweighed the bad.* TOP | *My dad and me with my grandfather Ezra "Pop" Carter. My son Jack Ezra carries on his namesake.* MIDDLE | *Dad with a nice catch on the banks of a wilderness river in Alaska.* ABOVE | *Family and friends, including my grandfather Ray (seated, in the red plaid) and uncle Roy (seated, in the black shirt), on a hunting trip to Kingsland, Arkansas, Dad's birthplace, in 1976. Dad's first cousin Mark Rivers (far left) still lives there and hunts the same land.*

the rest of his body obscured by the dark engine well. I heard a slam of metal on metal. "There's a cable undone back here; just can't get it back on." Again the metallic clanking sound, followed by another "Dag-gum!" Then came more grunting and finally a sigh of accomplishment. "There!" said Dad, exasperated. "Now give it a try."

As I went back to the wheel, I saw the little bird again, this time sitting on the port stern. I looked up and saw that the storm was now almost upon us, blowing our little boat about in what was now becoming a very rough sea. I sat down at the helm, said a prayer, and turned the key.

With a cough, the engine rumbled to life.

"Well, alright!" I heard Dad call from below.

He climbed out of the engine well and over to the helm, taking the wheel. And then we were off, as fast as our little boat could go, heading east.

I looked back to see if the little bird was still sitting on the stern of the boat, but it was gone. We went on, the sea beating at the sides of the boat, the wind beginning to pelt us with rain, the waves ever higher.

When we slowed the boat down because of the rising seas, a movement caught my eye. There out beside the boat I saw the little yellow bird, flying fast to keep up with us.

"The bird!" I cried.

Dad looked and sure enough, there was the little bird, flying right beside us.

"Dad! It wants to be on the boat with us!"

Dad smiled. "I am sure it will be just fine," he said.

I watched that little bird for the longest time as it flew just above the waves. The wind was gusting mightily now, and the rain was pelting down. Still the little bird continued beside our vessel, beating its tiny wings with all its strength.

We crested a great wave, and our boat crashed back down, the bow hitting the sea forcefully. We both fell forward, struggling to keep our balance. Dad straightened the boat back into the wind, which luckily was from the northeast that day, and we slowed even more.

When I looked up again the little bird was gone.

"Dad!" I cried. "The bird! The bird is gone! It went down in the waves!" Tears were beginning to well up in my eyes.

Over the roar of the wind he answered, "Son, that bird is fine. I am sure it was a guardian to watch over us. We are safe, now. The bird is gone on."

And so we kept on, and before long the wind began to die down, and with it, the tumultuous seas. As the clouds departed and the waves subsided, I saw that land was in fact not as far away as I had believed. Before long we were in the channel and soon at the dock. It was almost dark.

ABOVE | *My son Joseph, Dad, Rosanne, and my mother relax and play Carter Family music on the front porch of the Carter Family home in Hiltons, Virginia.*
OPPOSITE | *This is one of my father's most profound poems, which expresses his sense of persistence and duty.*

Brisbane, Aust
May 15th 1991

Dear You,

I shall not mourn for my lost youth
For I was born to know the truth
And to be realistic; face the facts
And not look down, and not look back
To let it be and let it roll
I try to keep me in control
To say and do as I am called
And trust there's life to do it all
Discernment to do all things well
And give right good and give wrong hell
I would be sure; I'd be discreet
To choose the path that takes my feet
Upon the paths that they should go
And know the signposts I should know
To gain each goal and do each task
As well as God or Man could ask
And all I ask is, At the end,
You could say to Women or Men
Just one thing I'd have you tell
"He knew his duty. He did it well."

John R. Carln

JOHNNY CASH

Dec 18 1983
Palm Spring

John Carter;

This arm band is a symbol to you that I have cut the old bad habits.

Please keep it for a souvenir.

This is a beautiful place to get well. Though I am lonely, I am happy here for the next month.

Have a wonderful Christmas, and take care of Mama.

Love Dad.

We had fried fish that night, made with my mother's recipe. It was wonderful. But as I lay down to sleep, exhausted and beaten by the sun, sea, and wind, I could not get that little bird out of my mind.

There were so many times when we were in dangerous places; so many times when I feared for my life. But I always felt safe. How is this so? I believed. Was the bird a guardian? Was I truly safe because of a spirit watching over us? Or was I safe with the man I trusted and believed in? Perhaps both. But maybe it was my dad's faith that reassured me, rather than my own. There were many times when I was uncertain and afraid. But Dad believed. His faith was strong.

A lesson taught with words and force is seldom learned. This I learned from Dad through his words and actions. I have learned my lessons in only two ways: by watching the example of others or through my own pains, my own wrong turns. No one could make me believe I was not on the right path if

I LEARNED FROM DAD THROUGH HIS WORDS AND ACTIONS.

I did not want to believe it. I had to take it and find out for myself. My father was the same way. Though he suffered many times from his addictions, bad choices, and bad living, he would return again and again to the same path, only to find the same results. It was many years before he made positive, lasting changes.

When I was suffering from addiction and in great emotional pain, I went to my father. In 1991, when I was barely twenty-one, I was lost and scared, depressed and needing help. Dad was never angry with me over my addiction, just hurt and concerned. He told me I had a great faith, that this faith was in my blood, and that my salvation was already determined. He reminded me of my ancestors, how my great-grandfather, grandfather, and he were all ordained ministers, and this faith in Christ was in my soul. In this I found strength and understanding. My father prayed with me that day. Both of us admitted that we were lost and alone, needed help, and needed each other. We prayed for God to give us strength, to show us His way. I believe that God was

---

OPPOSITE | *My dad sent me this letter in December of 1983 from the Betty Ford Center in Palm Springs. He'd arrived there after being checked into the Eisenhower Medical Center as William H. Overton.* ABOVE | *My dad and I heading to the Grammy Living Legends Awards Show in New York City in 1991. I'm pretty sure the limousine behind us is the same one I mention in Chapter One. We used the same driver and car for years.*

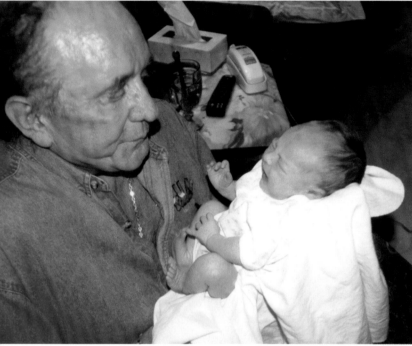

there with us that day, that He heard our prayer and that in his own way and time, He answered it.

But sadly, neither my nor my father's addictions passed immediately with that prayer. Before long I was as lost as I'd ever been. Within a year, my father and I both went to another drug treatment center, this time less than a month apart.

In the summer of 1992, Dad finished his in-treatment program and moved into a rental house, continuing his extended treatment. I came to join Dad at the house, and at his urging, I went in for evaluation and family therapy. I was pretending to be off drugs, but in reality was still using. I had stopped drinking, but was smoking grass and taking Xanax. I attended a group session at the center one day and expressed my great anger in front of the group, which came out in the form of incoherent ranting. I spoke out against the addiction in our family as if I was not experiencing it myself, as if I had been a victim. I went back to the rental house that evening in a huff.

The counselor, a tough, stern, and wise man, reached out to my father and told him of my outburst. Dad came to me that night and we had a long talk. I was no longer angry, but still I was upset. I also told him I had not been using drugs.

Dad knew better. Before he went to bed he put the letter shown on the facing page beneath my door.

After I read the letter, I was still angry. I immediately wadded up the paper and threw it in the wastebasket. I lay on the bed for a while, staring at the ceiling and sifting through my jumbled thoughts. Then I got up and took the paper out of the wastebasket and reread it. As I lay there, I pondered what the letter meant. It was a way of reaching me without pointing a finger, without judging me. His letter was truly a gift, a way to reach out and show unconditional compassion. The next day I checked myself into the treatment center.

Dad was open-minded and understanding because he had experienced what I was going through. He hoped that those he loved would not suffer the same pains and struggles that he had, but when we did, he supported and stood by us. He also had the ability to see the miracles in what appeared to be commonplace; his faith helped those who loved him find greater strength and purpose. So many of us looked up to him. And when we were troubled, we reached out to him, knowing we would never be denied his wisdom or unconditional love.

TOP | *Dad and I stand face-to-face at Laura's and my wedding.* MIDDLE | *Dad holding my daughter, Anna Maybelle.* ABOVE | *My parent's last portrait as a couple.* OPPOSITE | *This is the letter my father gave me in the summer of 1992, when I, too, was struggling with drugs. Each year of my life, the strength of my father's wisdom becomes more and more clear. I miss him dearly, though in many ways he is very much with me today.*

John C.

I'm not giving you this scripture to admonish you.

It's the one I read to you on the phone from Bou Aqua.

I needed to hear this more than you did.

Eccl: 5 2-3

"Be not rash with thy mouth and let not thine heart be hasty to utter anything before God: for God is in Heaven, and thou upon Earth: therefore let thy words be few.

For a dream cometh through a multitude of business; and a fools voice is known by multitude of words"

Love
Dad -

CHAPTER NINE

NEW BEGINNINGS & LEGACIES

A LTHOUGH DAD HAD NEVER STOPPED BEING CREATIVE, THE PUBLIC WAS JUST NOT CATCHING ON. HE WAS STILL SELLING TICKETS IN THE EARLY '90S, AND THE AUDIENCES STILL CHEERED. BUT HE WAS NOT ENJOYING ANY HITS, AND HE MISSED THE EXCITEMENT

of bringing out new material to critical acclaim. His audience seemed to be getting older and older.

Then in February 1993, a man with long hair and an even longer beard showed up backstage at the Rhythm Café in Santa Ana, California, where Dad was playing. His name was Rick Rubin. Dad's manager, Lou Robin, had come to Dad before the show to tell him that Rick wanted to talk to him afterward.

"I'd say he's just another record company guy who wants to sell his ideas to me, but I'll meet him and at least hear him out," Dad had answered without a lot of enthusiasm.

And so Rick came into Dad's dressing room and both men said hello. Then, according to Lou, Rick and Dad simply sat and stared at each other for two minutes or so, saying nothing and seeming to size each other up. Dad figured Rick was probably looking for an easy gig with an established artist,

but instead Rick proposed something Dad had always dreamed of but had never been offered: a simple recording plan. Come into the studio with me and make the music you have always wanted to make. Follow your heart, and record with a band or not. Sit in front of the microphone and sing your songs the way you want.

For Dad, this was a breath of fresh air compared to the options he could have found in Nashville or elsewhere from various producers. And so Dad signed the deal with Rick Rubin and his newly formed company, American Recordings. Dad went to Los Angeles and spent day after day at Rick's house, making the music his heart dictated.

Dad did record with a band some on that first trip to Rick's in 1993, but very little of that material was released. It was the simplest production, only voice and guitar, that was the focus of the first record with Rick,

---

THESE PAGES | *In the last years of his life, Dad reached a whole new fan base with the series of records he did with American Recordings. To many of his younger fans, these recordings defined who Johnny Cash was.*

I love the spirituals — wash all
my troubles away. — roll around
heaven all day.
   I could get lazy thinking
about it.   In Beverly Hills at Rick
Benmont played some nice key-
board, Mike Campbell on guitar. The
two of them together just carried
me away. I only sang the song once
and it felt right.
   I can't sing it without
thinking of the Arkansas Cotton
   Rick lies flat on his back
on the floor of the control room
While I'm recording at his house. His
dogs roam the room as they always
do when I'm recording.   (
   you'd think he's asleep but he
isn't. He hears every sound. He

titled *American Recordings*, like the company's name. The songs were a varied assortment, from the dark and mysterious "Thirteen" to Dad's heartfelt version of Kris Kristofferson's "Why Me Lord." But it was my father's arrangement of the old American murder ballad "Delia's Gone" that received the most acclaim. The video for the song, featuring the supermodel Kate Moss as the ill-fated young woman, portrayed my father as a dark and dangerous figure—her lover and her murderer. Americans loved it, including American youth, which was most exciting for my father. It wasn't long before Dad's career was on fire again.

Both *American Recordings* and its follow up, *Unchained*, featuring Tom Petty and the Heartbreakers as the backing band, won Grammy Awards. But country radio and Nashville in general did not pay much heed.

I was having a quiet dinner with my parents one evening in 1996, not long after Dad's *Unchained* had won the Grammy for Best Country Album. Winning was a big deal for sure. "Well, I talked to Billy [Graham] today," Dad announced. "Just after I got a call from Rick. Rick wants to take out an ad in *Billboard*."

He chewed. "What kind of ad?" I asked.

"The huge kind," he replied, spooning out the corn bread from his cup of buttermilk. "The kind that will rattle things. He wants to use the finger photo."

One of the most famous photographs in existence is the "bird shot," as we call it around the family. The photo, taken at one of the rehearsals for the live concert at San Quentin, captures my father's spirit at its rebellious best.

"I said no at first," Dad continued, "then I called Billy Graham. He didn't tell me to do it or not to do it, just that he wouldn't judge me either way. After my talk with him, I prayed about it and called Rick back. I gave him the go-ahead."

The advertisement read: "American Recordings and Johnny Cash would like to acknowledge the Nashville Music establishment and country radio for your support."

Of course, this ad really shook Nashville up. In many ways it was a wake-up call. Perhaps country music was broader and more expansive than the power brokers in Nashville had assumed. It was after this ad was placed that country radio program directors and record company executives all over the world took note. Many of them had it framed and put on permanent display in their offices. It became a reminder to stay open-minded and pay attention to what the people wanted—to facilitate, rather than direct the music business. It was after this ad appeared that the genre of Americana took root and became firmly established in our culture. This movement owes a great deal to my father's records on American Recordings.

Dad retired from the road in 1997 due to his illnesses, but this did not slow down his music. He recorded more and more. When Dad began work on *American III*, he asked me to join him in the studio. Dad wanted to record music in his log cabin near the House on the Lake in Hendersonville. He had set up a small recording system there a few years before and had put down some songs. Now he wanted to make it more of an operating studio.

In fact, the only extended period he wasn't in the studio was the time he spent at either of my parents' two peaceful vacation homes. One, in Jamaica, was the fabulous Cinnamon Hill Great House. Cinnamon Hill, overlooking the beautiful Caribbean Sea two miles below, was built in the first half of the eighteenth century by the Barrett family. At one time it was the family residence on a huge sugar cane plantation. The home was a safe haven to my parents, where they could truly rest, the gentle trade winds blowing up from the ocean.

OPPOSITE | *Dad was extremely excited about his work with Rick Rubin and kept detailed notes about their recording sessions. These are from the notebook he kept while working on* American IV: The Man Comes Around. ABOVE | *When* American IV *won a Grammy Award, Rick suggested an advertisement featuring this famous photograph be taken out in* Billboard, *thanking the Nashville music establishment and country radio for their support. Dad was never afraid to express his emotions or strong feelings, however he saw fit.*

The Best of Johnny Cash & June Carter

1. Allegheny
2. Darling Companion
3. Lifes Little ups and downs
4. What'd I Say?
5. Happy to Be With you
6. If I Were a Carpenter
7. Jackson
8. If I Had a Hammer
9. Pack Up your Sorrows
10. Old Time Feeling
11. It ain't Me Babe
12. Farside Banks of Jordan

The second home-away-from-home was the Carter Family ancestral home in Hiltons, Virginia. It was built by Ezra Carter in the 1930s. My mother could trace her heart roots to this place and reaffirm her faith. Dad loved it, too. They spent hour after hour on the front porch, writing, reading, and making music.

But Dad couldn't stay away from the studio for long.

And so Dad had his engineer David Ferguson buy a bit more gear and wire the cabin up for professional recording. Often, Rick came to Hendersonville to make music with Dad. I was there for almost all of these sessions and learned two things: when to keep my mouth shut and when to chime in with an opinion, though during the early recordings, I was more vocal than I needed to be. Rick is wonderful in the studio. He seems to know how to direct the session without being imposing—how to help the

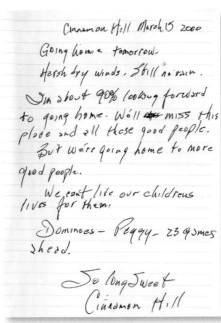

Cinnamon Hill March 15 2000
Going home tomorrow.
Harsh dry winds. Still no rain.
I'm about 90% looking forward to going home. We'll miss this place and all these good people. But we're going home to more good people.
We can't live our childrens lives for them.
Dominoes - Peggy - 23 games ahead.

So long Sweet Cinnamon Hill

process along without complicating things. I learned a great deal from Rick in those sessions.

My wife, Laura Cash (Laura Weber at the time), took part in some of those early recordings at the cabin. Dad loved her fiddle playing. She brought him a good few songs, including "I'm Free from the Chain Gang Now" and "The Evening Train." Laura remembers the first day she went into the studio with Dad. I was engineering. A friend and wonderful old-time guitar player named Larry Perkins (no relation to Luther Perkins, Dad's longtime guitar player), Laura, Dad, and I were the only ones there that day.

"The energy that day was intense," said Laura. "It was intimate and intimidating at the same time. It was so quiet in that room. There were candles lit and everything was peaceful, but I was nervous and in awe. It was the first time I'd ever been around him in that type of environment."

OPPOSITE | *One of Dad's song lists and album concepts, "The Best of Johnny Cash and June Carter."* TOP | *In this photo from 1975, my mother stands in front of my parents' Jamaica home, the majestic Cinnamon Hill Great House, built in 1747.* ABOVE | *In the latter years of their lives, my parents spent a great deal of time at Cinnamon Hill.*

We recorded a version of "Wayfaring Stranger" that day, another of Laura's suggestions. Laura and Larry accompanied Dad as he sang and played guitar.

"At first," said Laura, "I was playing lines with more notes. He said, 'play longer lines and fewer notes.' The next pass through he turned to me and said, 'How does it feel to play on a Grammy Award–winning album?' That was when I knew I had done something right. It felt like we were the only people on the face of the earth." The album did, in fact, go on to win a Grammy, just as Dad had predicted.

These sessions at the cabin went on for the rest of Dad's life. Some of the recordings for the remaining American albums were done at Rick's studio in California, but a great deal were recorded at what became known as Cash Cabin Studio. There were many great musicians who took part in these sessions, such as Randy Scruggs, Marty Stuart, Pat McLaughlin, Benmont Tench, Smokey Hormel, and Mike Campbell, to name a few. The recordings at the cabin carried on even when Rick wasn't there. David Ferguson, my brother-in-law Jimmy Tittle, and I facilitated the production as best we could.

Rick deserves a lot of credit for his work with Dad, but every producer who has worked with my father has admitted that Johnny Cash was not really produced—you just stood back and tried to capture what happened. Dad always had a vision for his projects, bringing his own songs and other favorites to the table. He had a unique ability to determine whether a song could work for him. And he was never wrong about it. When Rick brought Dad "Turn, Turn, Turn," by the Byrds, my father knew very well it was a wonderful song but decided quickly he would not record it. He said it was just not right for him. Alternatively, when Rick brought Dad "Hurt," he immediately knew it was a good choice. He took these songs, including "Personal Jesus," "Solitary Man," "Desperado," and the raucous "Rusty Cage" and made them his own. I brought my father a few good songs, though he passed on more than he recorded. But when I played him Sting's "I Hung My Head" and Bruce Springsteen's "Further On (Up the Road)," he immediately knew they would work for him.

There were many studio days that I remember well. On one occasion we were recording for *American IV* in Los Angeles at Rick's home studio, the Akademie Mathematique of Philosophical Sound Research. That week was very successful. Dad had already cut "Desperado," "Bridge Over Troubled Water," and some others that would later become a part of the final CD. Joe Strummer of the Clash had been

---

ABOVE | *Even when my father was seriously ill, he never gave up dreaming and not once lost his inspiration; if anything, he redoubled his efforts.*
OPPOSITE | *A song list my father made when recording* American IV.

1. Big Iron
2. I Came on
3. The Man
4. Wichita
5. I Hung my
6. One More
7. Gentle On
8. We'll Meet
9. For you
10. Streets of
11. Tear Stained
12. Day After
13. No Expec.
14. Bridge
15. Father and
16 Give My
17. First Time
18 Hurt
19. Per. Jesus
20. Sam Hall
21 Redemption
22 Desperado
23 Cindy
24 Lonesome
25 Never Walk
26 Danny

309

① had a woman
A while back
Down a long mainline
Down a short side track
Nothing could replace
This love of my mine
But Asthma coming down like the 309
Like the 309
Asthma coming down like the 309

309
② I like you
And you like me
And we're both as tight
As ABC
Come September
We will make some wine
But Asthma coming down
Like the 309
" " "
Asthma

309

Take me to the Depot
Put me to bed
Lay an electric fan
On my gnarly old head
Everybody take a look
To see Jim doin' fine
Then load my box on the 309
On the 309.....
Asthma comin down like the 309

Everytime I hear that whistle blow
I wonder can you hear it o' babe
And I wonder if you hear
This singin of mine
Asthma comin' down
Like the 309
Asthma comin' down

309

A chicken in the pot
And a turkey in the corn
Aint felt this good
Since Jubilee morn
Talk about luck
Well I got mine
Asthma comin down the 309
like the the 309
" " ' ' - '
Asthma coming down

Walkin down the track
Just singing a song
It should be awhile
Before the train comes along
A good way to end
This life by mine
Would be to be far out
By the 309

hanging out all week, and we began that day working with Joe. (Not long after this, Joe died of cancer.) Rick had suggested "One Love" by Bob Marley, but though Dad loved the song, he had determined it was not for him. Looking through the Marley repertoire we rediscovered "Redemption Song." Smokey Hormel sang the tracking vocal while a song was recorded. We continued this process the whole week, especially when Dad wasn't completely familiar with the song. We would find the right key for him and then someone would sing the live tracking vocal while Dad sat back and listened to the recording taking place, oftentimes offering input and direction. By the time we were through, Dad usually felt up to the task and would go in and sing the song a few times through—and generally did not need to sing it again.

After a particularly moving recording of the Marley song (which may be heard on the American Recordings' *Unearthed* box set), we decided to try the recording of "Hurt." I knew the song by heart, having been a fan of Nine Inch Nails for years. I sang it live with the band that day, and the experience will never leave me. I had the chance to be a part of the formulation of this recording with Smokey, Benmont, and Mike Campbell. What these musicians did was perfect for my father. It was like watching magic take place.

Immediately after we finished tracking the song, Dad went in and sang it.

That week we wrapped up *American IV* and went home, but Dad would not take a break. Within a few days, we were back in the studio working on *American V*.

During this recording process, Dad's health typically was not good. He was losing his sight, and his diabetes was sapping his strength. Dad probably had diabetes for many years and left it untreated. It was only the last year of his life that he accepted the disease and took steps toward treatment.

All this time, through these struggles, sicknesses, and triumphs, my parents' love for each other gave them both a lot of strength. They had ceased fighting altogether and never bickered in the least. They had come to accept each other unconditionally, and it showed in their everyday life. They were always affectionate and loving to each other. Somehow their love had not only endured but grown. My mother and father were each other's best friends.

I don't believe anyone, with the exception of my mother and possibly her doctor, knew the extent of her heart trouble. But my mother expressed a great peace in what seemed a conscious knowledge of her approaching end. I remember very clearly the last day I spoke to her in May 2003. She was

OPPOSITE | *Dad's song "Like the 309" shows his magical ability to laugh in the face of his own sickness and mortality. Just as the lyrics imply, Dad suffered from chronic asthma during the last years of his life.* ABOVE | *My wife, Laura, and I perform with my father onstage at the Carter Fold with family and friends.*

weak although smiling, going through her jewelry, picking out pieces to give away to her daughters and friends. She had a great sadness in her eyes that day, and yet along with the sadness was peace. She had come to terms with her life and was happy with it. I think my father also sensed Mom's life was winding down. Perhaps their joint realization had brought them closer together.

The next day Mom went to the hospital with chest pains, weakness, and difficulty breathing. Within a week, she was dead.

My father had lost his best friend, his other half. He was heartbroken. However, in the face of this greatest of life's pains, one he had not encountered with such intensity since losing his brother Jack, he did not stop. He kept recording. The first session Dad did after the funeral was a project I was producing as a tribute to the Carter Family, called *The Unbroken Circle*. The first song he recorded was a beautiful one called "I Found You Among the Roses"—as of now unreleased. Rick came for the sessions a few days later, during which we recorded "God's Gonna Cut You Down" and "Ain't No Grave Gonna Hold My Body Down."

It was as if in the grip of such great pain, all Dad could do was sing and find solace in his music. By the summer he was functionally blind. All his books sat on his shelf unread. This was another sadness. He could no longer pursue his lifelong passion for reading; even his Bible sat gathering dust on his desk. He was consumed by depression, to be sure, but he did not stop. To me this was a demonstration of the greatest courage. What greater work can there be than that which is done during such a trying time? Does this not define a person as even greater than the work done in the prime of life? What my father was made of was quite apparent during these last months of his life.

When it was announced that the video for the song "Hurt" was up for the Best Cinematography Award on the MTV Video Music Awards show, Dad refused to hear that he could not go. He was determined. He bought his ticket and we all planned to attend. But when the date approached, he fell ill and was forced to go into the hospital to deal with another bout of pneumonia. It was not his spirit that gave up in the end, but his body. If not for his physical illnesses, he would have carried on. Many say that my father died of a broken heart. I do not believe this is true. I believe he died with a broken heart, but it did not kill him.

After he got out of the hospital that time and came home, we were back in the studio. We had put on an addition to the cabin, and Dad was excited to use his new recording room. He cut his unforgettable "Like the 309," laughing in the face of illness right to the end.

I remember vividly the day my father was taken to the hospital for the last time. I had rushed over to the house from the cabin when I got the call he was very ill. I arrived just as the ambulance was about to pull out. I approached Dad, who had an oxygen mask over his face.

"I love you, Dad," I said. "You're gonna be just fine."

He did not respond, but I will never forget the look in his eyes. It was a look that said "not this time." I had seen this same look in my mother's eyes just a few months before.

That same night, my sisters Rosanne, Kathy, and I gathered around his bed and Dad passed out of this world and into the next. I believe his greatest emotion as he left this world was overwhelming excitement to see my mother's face again.

IT WAS NOT HIS SPIRIT THAT GAVE UP IN THE END, BUT HIS BODY.

So who was this man, this enigma? Who was he beneath the rugged exterior? How could he make us so easily believe he was either a devil or an angel, and sit beside the president one day and a farmer the next (and often did), equally at ease beside either one? How did he become this man, so deep and mysterious, yet so open and accessible, all at the same time?

Dad had a great love of nature and the outdoors, where he sometimes sought solitude. He spent long periods of time throughout his life alone. I believe it was his isolation, in part, that made us want to be closer to him, to comfort him and be comforted by him.

My father was continuously searching. He searched so far and long, carrying his loved ones with him on his quests.

OPPOSITE | *Dad never hesitated when it came to forging ahead and finding new and different musical ground. Here he goes over a song with Nick Cave (left), Smokey Hormel (center), and Rick Rubin (right).*

And we looked up to him, seeking his wisdom and guidance, though at times he admittedly could offer neither. And throughout his restless struggles, his loss and pain, if he had been asked "What are you looking for?" surely he would have answered with resounding truthfulness that he had found his treasure long, long before: his salvation from God. And yet he was never full.

Dad's influence on our musical culture is unequaled. His music can be heard in every corner of the planet. It is with honesty and an almost childlike self-effacement that he found a way into the public's heart, without even seeming to try.

I encounter him somewhere every day. I see him on the television and on the Internet, and I hear him on the radio. His life story has been immortalized on film, radio, and television. There are various documentaries, which air often. New fans are introduced to his life and music regularly through the film *Walk the Line*, which won many awards, including two Golden Globes plus an Oscar for Reese Witherspoon's portrayal of my mother.

When Larry King asked my father on his show what he would most like to be remembered for, Dad's initial and heartfelt response was that he would like to be remembered as a good father. In this, his legacy is safe. All my siblings and I remember him that way. There were, of course, times when he fell short, as we all do. But in the final analysis, the scales tip heavily in his favor, and the wounds have healed and been forgiven.

Every day, when people hear the steady boom-chicka-boom over a speaker in a public place and are introduced to the music of Johnny Cash, many are intrigued enough to learn more about his music. Upon investigation, those new fans find there is a lot of depth to the music and the man. It's something that continually impresses everyone who has known him. As we all look deeper, we may feel confused and intrigued. Then as we peel away the final layers and peek into the heart of all that may be known about the man, we discover his faith, his love for God, his passion for what is right, and his ultimate strength. God stood with him through it all. Dad was a tool for God's work. All the darkness and toughness amount to one thing: a lure to reel us in for a closer look so that when we see behind the illusion, we find a simple, kind man who had faith in God.

ABOVE AND OPPOSITE | *When my mother passed, a portion of my father went with her—they were closer and more in love then than ever before in their later years. But Dad never lost sight of what he believed in, never lost his passion. I believe that now their love is only that much greater.*

I'll Still Love You

One of these mornings
I'm gonna rise up flying
One of these mornings
I'll sail away beyond the blue
I've got a promise
That there's a better world ahead
I want you to know that when I go
~~I'm making you~~ I'll still love you

One of these mornings
When my troubles over
One of these mornings
When all my suffering is through
I'll go out singing
It'll be a day to sing about
And I guarantee for eternity
I'll still love you

I wont be a stranger
When I get to heaven
Cause you gave me heaven
Right here on earth
~~I wonder be~~ If I get rewarded
With a mansion on a golden street
I want you to know
For what its worth
I'll still love you

CHAPTER TEN

REFLECTIONS FROM FAMILY & FRIENDS

ONE OF MY FATHER'S FAVORITE SCRIPTURES WAS GALATIANS 5:22-23: "BUT THE FRUIT OF THE SPIRIT IS LOVE, JOY, PEACE, FORBEARANCE, KINDNESS, GOODNESS, FAITHFULNESS, GENTLENESS, AND SELF-CONTROL. AGAINST SUCH THINGS THERE IS NO LAW."

These qualities were characteristic of the friendship and love Dad gave to the people in his life. And though many of his best friends happened to be wealthy or celebrities, he never chose them based on their status.

One of my father's best friends in the world was a good man from Hickman County, Tennessee, named Luther Fleaner. Luther is retired now, though for years he worked at the Ford glass plant in Nashville and looked after Dad's farm in Bon Aqua, Tennessee. Luther and Dad spent a great deal of time together. When I was young, Luther would take Dad and me coon hunting, which to those who do not know, is the process of chasing howling coonhounds through the darkened woods with flashlights and guns. That is to say, we spent a lot of time sitting around a campfire and chewing tobacco. When the dogs began

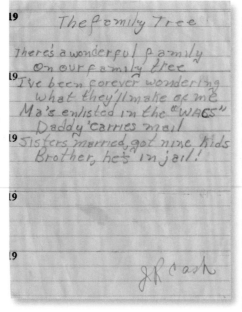

to "bay," meaning their howls became stationary, it was a sign they had run an animal up a tree—usually a possum. These were good, simple times where my father, Luther, and I really enjoyed ourselves. Dad loved Luther because they related at the level of the heart.

Some of Dad's dearest friends have passed away, including Dr. Nat Winston, Waylon Jennings, and John Rollins, but there are still a good few around. He is remembered fondly by so many—family members, dear friends, colleagues in the music industry, and those who simply love his music. On the following pages are a few reflections from some who were dear to my father, loved him throughout his life, and cherish their memories of the time they spent with him. He meant many different things to the people who contributed to this chapter, but they all loved him dearly.

ABOVE | *Family always meant the world to my father, though he jests about it in this early poem.* OPPOSITE | *Dad moved into the House on the Lake in 1967 by himself, though his daughters visited him often from California. Here he is shortly after the move with Cindy (left), Kathy (middle), Rosanne (right), and Tara (on his lap).*

LAURA CASH

My wife, Laura, is a spiritual, strong-natured, talented, and family-centered woman. When my mother and father met her, they were immediately attracted to her and saw her for just what she was: the real deal. But most important, my parents sensed that she would be a wonderful, loving, and caring mother to our children. Laura worked with Dad a few times in the studio, but she knew him mostly as our children's grandfather, which he took the utmost joy in always. —JCC

John Cash was a fantastic grandpa. He was gentle, patient, loving, and involved in his grandkids' lives. It was obvious that they brought him a great deal of joy.

There was a thing he did with the babies: He would tightly cradle them up against his chest and sing to them in his lowest voice, "Boom-bobba-boom-bobba-boom-ba-boom-baboom" over and over to a rockabilly-type rhythm. The vibration from his chest could be felt across the room. It would entrance the babe in his arms.

When our daughter, Anna Maybelle, was just over a year old, we were up in Virginia at the Carter family home, recording June's *Wildwood Flower* album. Anna Maybelle (AnnaBelle, as she likes to be called) was sitting on her grandpa's lap at supper, picking food off his plate. He always had a separate plate of sliced tomatoes and raw onions. She started eating those raw onions, and he just beamed with pride. "She's a Cash!" he said. I began to worry that the onions would make her sick, mixed with the bottle she just had. I said, "John, she's eating a lot of those onions, you may want to . . ." Before I could finish, he said, "Leave her alone, Mom," and offered her another piece. To this day raw onion is one of her favorite foods.

After June died, when AnnaBelle was two, we would take her to visit John often. She would make a beeline for his room, where she knew he would be. Before we could even get there ourselves, she was up in his lap, eating out of his stash of sugar-free milk chocolate. He would sit so patiently with her, as she would feed him little tiny champagne grapes, one at a time, for what seemed like hours. He would always perk up when he saw her.

John had an infectious youthful spirit, which really came alive when his grandchildren were around. I see John in the spirit of all of our children. Joseph spent a lot of time with him as a young child, and AnnaBelle as well. Jack, the namesake of John's adored brother, never got to meet his grandpa, but he may resemble his grandfather the most—he's mischievous, generous, and loving. His birthday is February 27, the day after his grandfather's birthday. —LAURA

OPPOSITE, CLOCKWISE FROM TOP LEFT | *My mother with my sister Carlene • Another photo of Dad and his expanded family from not long after he moved into the House of the Lake. Standing, from left to right: Cindy Cash, Rozanna "Rosie" Nix, Lorrie Davis (my aunt Anita's daughter), my mother, Kathy Cash, Rosanne Cash, and Dad. Seated, from left to right: Carlene Smith and Tara Cash. • Dad with my sister Tara. • Dad with my sister Kathy. • Left to right: Dad with his sister Joanne, sister Louise, and brother Roy in 1954.* ABOVE | *A current photo of me and my family. Left to right: Laura Cash, Jack Ezra Cash, me, Anna Maybelle Cash, Joseph John Cash.*

JOANNE CASH YATES

Joanne Cash Yates is my father's younger sister. She grew up, like all the Cash children, picking cotton in Dyess, Arkansas. Today, she is a pastor and spiritual advisor living in Hendersonville, Tennessee. Her husband, Harry Yates, is also a pastor. —JCC

Johnny was six years older than me, but being raised in cotton country, age didn't matter; we all worked side by side every day. Johnny (JR to me) was just my brother. We did everything together, all of us. We worked, played, went to church, but most of all, I remember the singing. We sang in the cotton fields, in church, and around Mama's old upright piano every night, as Mama played. We listened to the radio as much as possible, until Daddy told us to turn it off to save the battery! JR was *always* writing songs.

After Jack died, we became closer than ever before. JR was always gentle, and he never said an unkind word to me that I can remember. He was always there for me. JR said to me when I was ten or twelve, "Try to always do things right." He also said Jesus loved me, and then he said, "I love you, too." Another time he told me, "Sing with all your heart and as long as you can. You can do anything as long as you let Jesus guide you," and then he looked at me with his magical grin and gave me a hug. In my life now, I miss him so very much, but the memory of the many things he told me are with me daily, and I will treasure these gifts for the rest of my life. —JOANNE

CINDY CASH PANETTA

Cindy Cash is my sister, Dad's third daughter. Right now she lives in Ventura, California, but is considering moving back to Hendersonville. —JCC

I was nine years old when my mother and father divorced. Dad moved to Nashville and Mom remained in Ventura. I spent the next nine years yearning for my dad. Although I was close with my mother, my heart ached, and I had an ardent desire to know my father better, to be close to him.

In 1977, when I was eighteen and newly divorced with a baby girl, I received a call from Dad urging me to move to Tennessee. I spent the next twenty-three years in Hendersonville, Tennessee, and Dad and I became very close. I was the epitome of a daddy's girl and loved it. He became the dad I had missed through those years, my confidante and the person I depended on for all of life's lessons.

In 1990, Dad and I were in a counseling session together. Long story but short answer. The therapist had asked us to sit facing one another, knees to knees. She asked Dad to name the one thing he appreciated most about me. His answer spoke volumes to me and showed me a side of Dad that I remained fiercely protective of. His response was, "I've never had to doubt for a second that Cindy truly loves me."

I remember little else of that day. —CINDY

ABOVE LEFT | *A photo from 1955 of a young and beautiful Joanne Cash from my grandmother Carrie's photo album.* ABOVE RIGHT | *Dad and my sister Cindy were great friends and connected in many ways.*

TOMMY CASH

Tommy Cash is my father's younger brother. Tommy is a successful performer and musician in his own right. As children growing up in Dyess, Arkansas, Tommy and Dad were close, though separated by eight years. Dad always referred lovingly to Tommy as his kid brother. —JCC

John told me, "Always follow your dreams. Don't let anything stand in your way." He also advised me, "Don't let people who ask you constantly, 'Are you really Johnny's brother?' bother you to the point to where it affects your goals." So I tell people who ask, "I knew Johnny like a brother." He was big brother to me long before he was Johnny Cash. —TOMMY

ABOVE | *My dad and I with my grandfather Ray (right) and Uncle Tommy Cash (left) in 1976.*

ROSANNE CASH

I have looked up to my sister Rosanne my entire life. She is strong and has been guided by her sense of morality and independent spirit throughout her life. Her music is her own and her artistry, unequaled. From the time I was young, I recall her laughter filling the house. I cherish her now as my oldest sibling and respect her to the utmost. When my mother passed, Rosanne gave up her life for at least a month and moved in with Dad to stay close. She was there for him during that time, supporting him and selflessly giving of her heart. For this, as our father was, I will always be grateful. —JCC

When I was nineteen years old, I was lying on my bed reading a book, and my dad walked into the room. "What are you reading?" he asked. I showed him the cover. "It's a book on astrology," I said. I waited for a sign of disapproval, but he just nodded. I pushed it a bit: "You don't believe in this, do you?" I asked. "No," he said, "but I think you should find out everything you can about it." His attitude was so generous and that sentence was so loving and spontaneous, that I was instantly filled with love and a giddy sense of liberation.

That was my dad in a nutshell, and that was his style of parenting. He treated people with respect; he encouraged curiosity; he reveled in freedom, and wanted others to do the same. And he had a basic belief that everyone had a right and an obligation to examine their own ideas, beliefs, principles, and opinions. He didn't judge, and he thought the world could accommodate a lot of very different people. It was the best lesson in parenting I could possibly receive and a graceful example of how to treat everyone.

I've never forgotten it, and today I remind myself to ask my children for their opinions, to listen to their crazy ideas, even to watch them reject what I hold dear, without judgment, so that they might find out who they are, what they believe, and what they love. That little exchange between Dad and me gave me confidence and a feeling that I could be self-determined and that my curiosity was welcome, even essential. I don't think he ever knew how important that moment was to me. I filed it away in a corner of myself, and I let it grow and change me until it was so much a part of the fabric of my own psyche that it seemed unnecessary and redundant to put words to it. But today, without my dad in this wide world, about which he was so curious, and in which he took up so much space with such grace, I wish I had told him how grateful I was for a single sentence he said to me when I was a teenager, when he was just being himself, when he was curious about what I was doing with my mind, when he wanted me to find out everything I could about everything. —ROSANNE

OPPOSITE | *Dad and Rosanne at the Memphis Zoo in 1956. Rose was one year old.* ABOVE | *Rosanne is one of the most grounded and astute people I know.*

THE ROLLINS FAMILY

John and Michele Rollins were longtime friends of my parents. We spent a great deal of time in Jamaica with the Rollins family growing up. Their children, Michael, Monique, Mark, and Michele, and John's older son, Ted, were all my parents' godchildren. Unlike the many people in my parents' lives who tugged at them and demanded things of them, the Rollins family spent time with my parents simply because they enjoyed their company. —JCC

MICHELE ROLLINS

Johnny Cash, the man, the singer, the composer, the legend: I took those things for granted when I met him in 1976 backstage at Wolf Trap, in Virginia.

During a financial downturn for my husband, John Rollins, Johnny bought Cinnamon Hill Great House as a show of support, but more importantly, as a show of friendship. As is so often the case, gestures from the heart bring much happiness. Cinnamon Hill became a resting place, a place of solace and rejuvenation, and a place of joy and music where the private Johnny Cash enjoyed time with his soul mate, June, and spent time reading about the things that meant so much to him: history, geography, philosophy, and so much more.

I was always struck by the generosity of spirit demonstrated by Johnny and June, very uncommon to stars of their caliber. There were no young talents they didn't support by allowing them to appear on their live show. Never mind that they allowed my guitarist son, Ted; flute-playing son, Michael; and daughter, Monique, a singer, to be in the show repeatedly. After all, they were godparents to all of our children. But the list of those very talented stars who got their start with Johnny and June is well known; some became legends in their own right.

When John Rollins died in 2000, there was a hole in my heart I thought would never heal. And when Johnny and June died so soon after in 2003, I wondered if my heart could ever fill with joy again. But when I look around and see my children and grandchildren, so full of the love my John and Johnny and June gave them, my broken heart is restored. —MICHELE

MICHAEL ROLLINS

Writing this is difficult for me because it means acknowledging he is gone. The echoes of his voice are still around me. He was consistently open and honest, as much as anyone I have ever known. I felt like I could ask him anything. Thinking of him reminds me that imperfection can be so much more refreshing and interesting. He never claimed to be a saint, and he helps me see, to this day, that a single mistake is not the end of the world but the basis of who you become. I knew of many of the mistakes he had made, of his addiction. His life was an open book to me—a book that I wish I had inquired more deeply into. And now the more I think of him, the more I write, the closer I feel to him. I guess this is how love works. —MICHAEL

TED ROLLINS

One of the most important things that JR said to me was after my father died. In his low, calm voice he said rather matter-of-factly, "Ted, you know when a parent dies that means a couple of things; you take on all of their good qualities, and you have a special angel up in heaven to watch out over you." I have carried those words with me since that day.

When I was much younger (and even more impressionable), we were walking somewhere one day, and part of the walk was through a restricted area. I said to him, "John, you know we aren't supposed to be going through here." And he replied, "If you just throw your shoulders back, walk fast, and act like you are supposed to be here, no one will ever bother you."

John to me was freedom from the ordinary, freedom from the bonds of normalcy. He taught me the importance and joy found in the little things, like frying ham in the morning or a good fire—or blowing things up. He was a great teacher and a very patient one at that. I always felt he understood me and that he had a deep insight into all the craziness in my life—good and bad. —TED

OPPOSITE, TOP LEFT | *Dad and mom were longtime friends with John and Michele Rollins and their family—really like extended godparents to all their children. Clockwise from top left: John Rollins, Michele Rollins, Michele Rollins, Mark Rollins, Monique Rollins, my niece Tiffany Lowe (Carlene Carter's daughter), Dad, Mom, and Michael Rollins.* OPPOSITE, TOP RIGHT | *Dad and his godson Ted Rollins stand back to back.* OPPOSITE, BOTTOM LEFT | *The Cinnamon Hill Great House.* OPPOSITE, BOTTOM RIGHT | *One of the many immigration cards my father filled out while traveling to Jamaica.*

JAMAICA IMMIGRATION CARD

Please print (press firmly).

RECORD THIS NO. IN A SAFE PLACE → ADMISSION No. 7799712

VISITORS ARE REQUIRED TO PRESENT THIS CARD ON ARRIVAL AND DEPARTURE. IT SHOULD THEREFORE BE KEPT IN A SAFE PLACE. IN CASE OF LOSS REPORT CARD NO. TO IMMIGRATION IMMEDIATELY.

1. Name: JOHN R CASH

2. Sex — M ☑ F ☐   3. Date of Birth 26 2 32

I.D. No. or
4. Passport No. 010948246 5. Type P

Place
6. of Birth Arkansas

7. Occupation Entertainer 8. Nationality USA

9. Permanent Address 200 CAUDILL

Hendersonville Tn 37075

10. Purpose of Travel Vacation 11. Length of Stay 16 days 12. FIRST VISIT Yes ☐ No ☐

ARRIVING PASSENGERS | DEPARTING PASSENGERS

13. Port of Embarkation MIAMI Flt EA No 979 | 14. Port of Disembarkation Flt. No.

15. Countries visited during last six weeks Germany England | 16. Last Address in Jamaica

Intended Address
17. in Jamaica CINNAMON Hill Rose Hall St Jmes

Signature: John R Cash | Signature:

FOR OFFICIAL USE ONLY

PERMITTED TO LAND IN JAMAICA ON CONDITION THAT THE HOLDER REMAINS NOT LONGER THAN AND DOES NOT ENGAGE IN ANY FORM OF EMPLOYMENT IN THE ISLAND OR SOLICIT OR ACCEPT ANY ORDER FOR GOODS OR SERVICES, FOR OR ON BEHALF OF ANY PERSON, FIRM OR COMPANY NOT CARRYING ON BUSINESS WITHIN THE ISLAND

ARRIVAL STAMP | DEPARTURE STAMP

IMMIGRATION OFFICER No. 117 01 JUN 1998 LANDED

EXTENSIONS:

KRIS & LISA KRISTOFFERSON

Kris Kristofferson was one of my father's closest friends, truly more like a brother. When Kris first met Dad, my father knew immediately he was something special, although at the time he was a janitor at a recording studio. My father saw Kris's vision and loved him for his spirit and his passion. Dad perceived in Kris a man who was not afraid to stand up for what he believed in, and in this they were very much alike. Kris and my father worked together on many occasions. In the mid-1980s they collaborated with Waylon Jennings and Willie Nelson as the Highwaymen. But it was as friends that Dad and Kris's relationship was strongest. —JCC

KRIS KRISTOFFERSON

Of the many blessings in my life, perhaps the greatest—aside from my family—is that so many of my heroes have become my close friends, beautifully enriching my time on the planet. I'm especially grateful to Johnny Cash for helping me become who I want to be.

The exhilarating electricity of his handshake backstage at the Grand Ole Opry put the final nail in the coffin of my military career. And his subsequent encouragement of my songwriting during my years as a janitor at the recording studio (he carried the lyrics to one of my songs in his wallet) were all I needed. Four years later, his recording of "Sunday Morning Coming Down," which I had written, won the Country Music Association's Song of the Year. And even before that, the door was always open at his house on the lake to me and a few of my songwriter friends. When I was working on the off-shore oil rigs in the Gulf, he made me famous in the oil fields when he called to tell me Luther Perkins, John's guitarist from 1955 through 1968, had died. Later, he put me onstage with him at the Newport Folk Festival (against their wishes), and I never had to work a day job again. The next thing I knew, I was standing next to him onstage performing all over the world with the Highwaymen.

The only advice I can remember him giving me was at Newport, when he said, "Try to sing louder. I can barely hear you in the room." It was the honesty and the power of his performance that showed me what to aim for. Aside from my wife and kids, he's the greatest blessing in my life. —KRIS

Lisa Kristofferson was a close friend to my parents for many years and spent a great deal of time with my mother and father. Her children knew my parents as an aunt and uncle, and Mom and Dad were also the godparents of the Kristoffersons' son, Johnny. Lisa is one of the strongest people I know, tough and loving. Like my mother, she considers family closeness the most important thing in life. When my mother passed away and I was in my worst pain, Lisa was there beside me, undaunted, comforting, and giving. I will always cherish her for that. —JCC

LISA KRISTOFFERSON

I was two months pregnant with our second son, Jody, when Kris and I were invited to Montreaux, Switzerland, to participate in *The Johnny Cash Christmas Special*, along with Willie and Connie Nelson and Waylon and Jessi Jennings. It was here that I was first introduced to the tradition of the songwriter's circle. Willie, Waylon, John, and Kris took turns with June and Jessi filling in any harmony gaps. I was moved to tears many times, and June asked me to chime in whenever I wanted. I made a joke about how I am the one person in my family who was told that I shouldn't sing, not even in the shower. Johnny looked right through me and said, "That may be true, but we performers hear ourselves through your eyes and we need that." He gave me a purpose: I could listen with awe and respect, and that's what I did for the next fifteen years of my life as I toured with the Highwaymen.

There are so many times during those years that John directed us back to what was real and what was important. Maybe because he had the wisdom as the eldest of the Highwaymen, but also because what he said always rang true, like the voice of God. He always remembered to say "I love you" and *always* said your name afterward: "I love you, Lisa." But it wasn't just that—he seemed *always* to mean it, too.

Toward the end of his life, on one of his reentries into the hospital, I had each of our kids write a get-well letter to him. He called when he received them and said that he had never received letters that meant more to him—not from presidents or kings. Children were his absolute joy. After June's funeral, I saw him swarmed by his grandchildren and smiled. Despite his failing health and immeasurable grief, the kids were there to keep him strong. —LISA

OPPOSITE | *Dad and Kris were like brothers. They laughed together and always enjoyed each other's company as artists and as the dearest of friends.*

LOU ROBIN

Lou Robin was Dad's manager for most of their respective careers. He continues to manage the Cash estate and protect my father's legacy. All those years I traveled with my father on the road show playing guitar and singing my part, Lou was there on every tour. He is one of the toughest men I know—determined and sharp, always looking out for Dad's best interests, and now, looking after his legacy. For many years Dad did not even have a contract with Lou, just a handshake agreement. —JCC

My company, Artists Consultants Productions, Inc., began promoting Johnny Cash concerts in 1969 and then progressed to the management position in 1973.

My relationship with John gave me the greatest respect for his genius as a composer, artist, and poet. His instinct when making decisions about his music and other business matters was uncanny. John was always honorable in his dealings. Despite his shortcomings, John was concerned about his fellow man. He was also that rare entertainer who could thrill audiences throughout the world the moment he took the stage.

Something John said to me once while we were traveling through Germany made a big impression, giving me a glimpse of a different side of the man: "Hey Lou! We need to cancel the shows tonight and tomorrow. John Carter (then age four or five) wants to go see some castles."

My life was profoundly affected by the wisdom gained from the many years I spent with John on and off the road. Having known him, it is fascinating to see his influence on young and old alike through his music and writings. I'm sure this will continue to be so for generations to come. —LOU

JACK SHAW

Rev. Jack Shaw was a friend and confidante for many years, traveling on Dad's road show and offering spiritual support and guidance. During the time Jack was on the road with us, we had a devotional before each show. We would all hold hands in a quiet corner of the backstage area (which was not always easy to find) and pray. —JCC

In 1993 John and I were in Branson, Missouri, talking backstage one evening. Just before the show started, he said, "Call me every day, Jack." "Every day?" I asked. "Every day. Around ten in the morning or seven in the evening." It was the most important thing he'd ever said to me.

For many years that followed, I did exactly that. Whether we were at home or on the road, on different floors in a hotel, or on opposite sides of the world, I would call him every day. Those calls were so precious. We'd discuss a variety of subjects as good friends do: problems, concerns, family, health, challenges—so many things. But ultimately, no matter the subject, we would end up discussing something spiritual, usually faith in the midst of adversity. We would talk about the Bible and what God's Word might have to say to us about heaven, loved ones who had passed away, or a favorite or particular verse.

John was compassionate to all and especially those down and out. He was strong in character (although a bit shy), fully committed to what he believed in, and an extremely bright and gifted individual. Often, when facing life's problematic challenges and/or difficulties, I ask myself, "What would John do; how would he conduct himself in this situation?" And, truly, doing so usually brings a perspective into focus that had not been there before.

John often said, "One of these days I'm going to set down and talk to Paul." One day I shall do likewise, but I must admit I am most excited about someday once again sitting down and talking to John. —JACK

ABOVE LEFT | *Lou Robin and my father about to descend into an Australian Opal mine in 1975. There was never a time in their relationship that Dad didn't trust Lou 100 percent.* ABOVE RIGHT | *Dad and his spiritual advisor Jack Shaw onstage in Branson, Missouri.* OPPOSITE | *I never saw my father or mother act ungraciously toward a fan.*

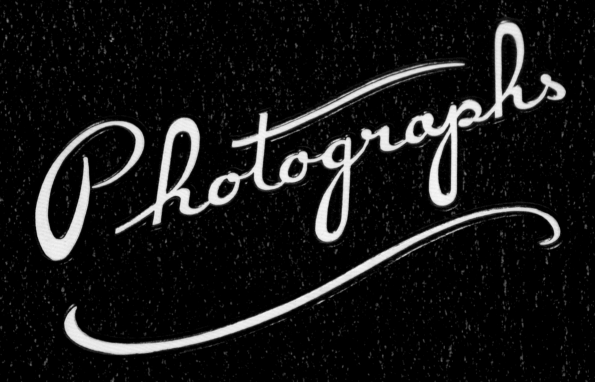

*Mom and Dad were married on March 1, 1968, in a small town in Kentucky.
I see the joy in their eyes in these photos and the promise of a new life to come.*

Dad and his mother, Carrie, at her work desk at The Johnny Cash Museum.
Grandma Carrie worked the last ten years of her life at Dad's museum in Hendersonville, Tennessee.

My grandfather Ray loved to laugh. I never saw my father disrespect him in any way.

Bandmates and crew hoist Dad into a jacuzzi.

Dad posing on drummer W.S. "Fluke" Holland's racing boat, The Ring of Fire.

Dad and longtime friend Marty Robbins joking around in the studio.

Clowning around again, this time with a Canada Trust ATM card in his mouth. In 1985, Canada Trust ran a campaign featuring the Johnny Cash Money Machine.

JACK CLEMENT

Jack Clement was one of my father's best friends, confidantes, and a producer of his music for many years. They were just plain silly together. Jack and Dad first met in Memphis in the mid-fifties, while Jack was the engineer at Sun Records. —JCC

I am very happy and proud that I got to spend a lot of time with Johnny Cash in a lot of places: Memphis, Nashville, New York City, Hawaii, Jamaica, Australia, Ireland, Scotland, England, Germany, and several other spots. Working with John was always fun, inspiring, and musical. I miss him every day. —JACK

MY FRIEND, THE FAMOUS PERSON
by Jack H. Clement

My friend, the famous person, is a barrel full of fun,
a rather shy guy, a very nice guy,
in spite of all he's done.
He's been around, this friend of mine,
ten times ten and then again.
Down the river 'round the world
and up the creek times ten.

For springing back brings secret laughter
and toughens up the chinny-chin
and lets the player fall down harder
just to get to bat again.
To really know a fellow person takes a while, you know;
it's seldom easy but easily worth it
just to find a kindred soul.
A kindred soul will pass the test or flunk it just for spite;
just to enjoy being a human,
so let him do it—it's his right.

Scold him quickly if he needs it
and never be a yes-ing man;
tell him no when no's the answer

or a lie he'll love and understand.
A kindred soul comes back around
and never really leaves;
though some time may pass
while he seems like an ass,
he'll show up in one of your dreams.

My friend, the famous person,
is a pal you might know, too,
for he has a lot of friends
and that's what makes him true.
A true friend will realize
there's more to the truth
than absence of lies.
It takes a good man to take success
and not misplace his soul
while bumbling through the facts of life
and too much rock and roll.
He's a hero still drifting upward,
ever rising 'cross the land,
ever learning, ever earning
my attention span.

OPPOSITE, TOP | *Dad and Jack Clement lean out of Jack's office window. They were forever joking around.* OPPOSITE, BOTTOM | *Norman Blake (right), Dad, and me on the front porch of the Cash Cabin Studio in Hendersonville, Tennessee.*

COLOPHON

Publisher: Raoul Goff
Acquiring Editor: Jake Gerli
Editor: Kate Etue
Production Editor: Jan Hughes
Art Director: Jason Babler
Designer: Michel Vrána
Production Director: Anna Wan

Insight Editions would like to extend additional thanks to Barbara Genetin, Christine Kwasnik, and Binh Matthews.

ABOUT THE AUTHOR

John Carter Cash has been surrounded by music his whole life, writing songs and staying active in the creative process. He is the only son of John R. Cash and June Carter Cash. He preserves the family legacy and is caretaker to the heritage of his musical ancestors.

A successful music producer, John Carter has been a producer on five Grammy Award–winning albums, including his mother June Carter Cash's *Press On* (1999), and has worked with Rick Rubin as Associate Producer on his father's *American III: Solitary Man* and *American IV: The Man Comes Around*, the latter receiving three Country Music Association awards. He owns and operates the Cash Cabin Studio and Cash Productions, LLC, near Nashville, Tennessee.

John Carter is the author of *Anchored in Love: An Intimate Portrait of June Carter Cash*, a biography of his mother, as well as several children's books.

Cash lives with his wife, Laura, and their three children in Hendersonville, Tennessee.

www.johncartercash.com

AUTHOR'S ACKNOWLEDGMENTS

Acknowledgments are due to those who were a part of the making of this book. First, I offer thanks to God for being my strength. Thanks to my editor, Kate Etue, for sticking with this and having faith. I am grateful to Jake Gerli and everyone at Insight Editions for seeing the possibilities for this book and helping to make it a reality. Thanks to Deborah Kops for the painstaking copyediting and to Michel Vrána for the wondrous design work.

Great thanks to Lou Robin, who still maintains and manages the Johnny Cash estate. Lou is the ultimate watchdog and stays true to my father's morals and goals, the same now as when the man was alive. He was an important sounding board for me throughout the process of putting this book together.

Special thanks to those who contributed: Billy Graham, Rosanne Cash, Lisa and Kris Kristofferson, Cindy Cash Panetta, Tommy Cash, Joanne Cash Yates, Michael and Michele Rollins, Ted Rollins, Jack Shaw, and "Cowboy" Jack Clement. Thanks to Allison McCoury and Lauren Moore for the invaluable organizational skills and patience, and to Kyle Gregory, Tom and Geri Moore, and Lisa Trice. Thanks to Maury Scobee, Marty Stuart, Chance Martin, Daniel Coston, Alan Messer, Amelia Davis, and Annie Leibovitz.

And my utmost gratitude to my wife, Laura Cash, who stuck with me through the writing and is always there, through it all.

And to Mark Stielper, who puts the utmost care and love into anything he does. Thanks for the invaluable help and for watching my back.